Reconciling Our Aims

The Berkeley Tanner Lectures

The Tanner Lectures on Human Values, which honor the American scholar, industrialist, and philanthropist Obert Clark Tanner, are presented annually at each of nine universities in the United States and England. They were established at the University of California, Berkeley, beginning in the 2000/2001 academic year. This volume is the fifth in a series of books based on the Berkeley Tanner Lectures. In this volume we include the lectures that Allan Gibbard presented in March 2006, along with the responses of the three invited commentators on that occasion—Michael Bratman, John Broome, and F. M. Kamm—and a final rejoinder by Professor Gibbard. The volume is edited by Barry Stroud, who also contributes an introduction. We have established the Berkeley Tanner Lectures Series in the belief that these distinguished lectures, together with the lively debates stimulated by their presentation in Berkeley, deserve to be made available to a wider audience. Additional volumes are now in preparation.

Robert Post
Samuel Scheffler
Series Editors

Volumes Published in the Series

Joseph Raz, *The Practice of Value*
Edited by R. Jay Wallace
With Christine M. Korsgaard, Robert Pippin, and Bernard Williams

Frank Kermode, *Pleasure and Change: The Aesthetics of Canon*
Edited by Robert Alter
With Geoffrey Hartman, John Guillory, and Carey Perloff

Seyla Benhabib, *Another Cosmopolitanism*
Edited by Robert Post
With Jeremy Waldron, Bonnie Honig, and Will Kymlicka

Axel Honneth, *Reification: A New Look at an Old Idea*
Edited by Martin Jay
With Judith Butler, Raymond Geuss, and Jonathan Lear

Reconciling Our Aims

In Search of Bases for Ethics

ALLAN GIBBARD

With Commentaries by
MICHAEL BRATMAN
JOHN BROOME
F. M. KAMM

Edited and Introduced by
BARRY STROUD

2008

OXFORD
UNIVERSITY PRESS

Oxford University Press, Inc., publishes works that further
Oxford University's objective of excellence
in research, scholarship, and education.

Oxford New York
Auckland Cape Town Dar es Salaam Hong Kong Karachi
Kuala Lumpur Madrid Melbourne Mexico City Nairobi
New Delhi Shanghai Taipei Toronto

With offices in
Argentina Austria Brazil Chile Czech Republic France Greece
Guatemala Hungary Italy Japan Poland Portugal Singapore
South Korea Switzerland Thailand Turkey Ukraine Vietnam

Published by Oxford University Press, Inc.
198 Madison Avenue, New York, NY 10016

www.oup.com

Oxford is a registered trademark of Oxford University Press

Library of Congress Cataloging-in-Publication Data
Gibbard, Allan.
Reconciling our aims : in search of bases for ethics / Allan Gibbard;
with commentaries by Michael Bratman, John Broome, F. M. Kamm;
edited and introduced by Barry Stroud.
p. cm.
Includes bibliographical references and index.
ISBN 978-0-19-537042-3
1. Ethics.   2. Utilitarianism.   3. Ethical intuitionism.
I. Stroud, Barry.   II. Title.
BJ354.G532R43 2008
170'.42—dc22   2007050470

1 3 5 7 9 8 6 4 2

Printed in the United States of America
on acid-free paper

Contents

REPLY TO COMMENTATORS

Allan Gibbard

List of Contributors

ALLAN GIBBARD is Richard B. Brandt Distinguished University Professor of Philosophy at the University of Michigan, Ann Arbor. He has been President of the Central Division of the American Philosophical Association and is Member of the American Philosophical Society, Membre Titulaire of the Institut International de Philosophie, Fellow of the American Academy of Arts and Sciences, and Fellow of the Econometric Society. He is the author of *Wise Choices, Apt Feelings* (1990), *Thinking How to Live* (2003), and numerous articles both in ethical theory and in such fields as theory of social choice, decision theory, evolutionary moral psychology, philosophy of mind and language, and epistemology.

MICHAEL BRATMAN is U. G. and Abbie Birch Durfee Professor in the School of Humanities and Sciences and Professor of Philosophy at Stanford University. He is the author of *Intention, Plans, and Practical Reason* (Cambridge: Harvard University Press, 1987; Reissued by CSLI Publications, 1999), *Faces of Intention: Selected Essays on Intention and Agency* (New York: Cambridge University Press, 1999), *Structures of Agency: Essays* (New York: Oxford University Press, 2007), and various other articles in the philosophy of action and related fields.

JOHN BROOME is White's Professor of Moral Philosophy at the University of Oxford. He was previously Professor of Philosophy at the University of St. Andrews and Professor of Economics at the University of Bristol. His books include *Weighing Lives* (1991), *Counting the Cost of Global Warming* (1992), *Ethics Out of Economics* (2001), and *Weighing Lives* (2004).

F. M. KAMM is Littauer Professor of Philosophy and Public Policy, Kennedy School of Government, and Professor of Philosophy, Department of Philosophy, Harvard University. She is the author of *Intricate Ethics* (2007), *Morality, Mortality*, vols. 1 and 2 (1992, 1996), *Creation and Abortion* (1992), and numerous essays on normative ethical theory and practical ethics.

BARRY STROUD is Willis S. and Marion Slusser Professor of Philosophy at the University of California, Berkeley. He is the author of *Hume* (1977), *The Significance of Philosophical Scepticism* (1984), *The Quest for Reality* (2000), and two volumes of collected essays on a variety of philosophical subjects.

Reconciling Our Aims

Introduction

BARRY STROUD

Allan Gibbard delivered the 2006 Tanner Lectures on Human Values at the University of California, Berkeley. Michael Bratman, John Broome, and Frances Kamm responded to the lectures as given and contributed energetically to three sessions of lively discussion. The lectures have been revised and expanded for publication, and the responses accordingly redeployed, and Allan Gibbard has replied in detail to his commentators. This book is the product of this fruitful philosophical interchange.

The lectures are directed first toward better understanding of the kind of thinking we all engage in when we deliberate and assess alternatives and decide what to do and then do it. It is Allan Gibbard's hope that the proper understanding of those ways of thinking can actually help us answer questions of what we ought to do or what is right or wrong in everyday social and political life. He is optimistic because part of his goal in answering the first question is to explain how a system of values best serves us or what makes morality of value to us in the world as we find it. He thinks moral or evaluative payoff is to be expected from the right kind of account of the nature of human practical reasoning.

Human beings are inevitably faced with questions of what to do and how to behave with one another. The fundamental idea from which Gibbard starts is that we cannot answer such practical questions solely by appeal to anything that could be found to be so in the natural world we all live in. We ask what we *ought* to do, but we ask it in a world that simply *is* the way it is; it is the world described by the natural sciences. To think that answers to such questions can be discovered by awareness or "intuition" of truths about what is to be done or what is best raises the question of how there can be such truths and how we are able to discover them. They could not be truths of the natural world as described by science. Gibbard has a different explanation of our having the practical convictions we all have.

Although answers to our practical questions cannot be found in the natural world, it *is* part of the natural world that human beings ask and answer such questions and act accordingly. So any study of how they do that, and of what kind of thinking it takes to settle the practical questions they face, will be a study of something that is part of nature. It is the particular kind of answer Gibbard wants to give to these factual questions about human beings that he thinks can make certain answers to human practical questions about what to do or what we ought to do more plausible than certain others.

It might seem obvious that when we reach a conclusion about what we ought to do in a particular situation, we have then come to think or believe that we ought to do such-and-such. Accepting that conclusion, we might also realize that if that is what we ought to do, then there is something else we ought to do first, and so conclude that we ought to do that other thing first. The obvious validity of such reasoning seems best accounted for by the fact that if the two premises we accept are true, it must be true that we ought to do that other thing first. Gibbard rejects the primacy of this kind of account of the validity, but without rejecting the obviously sound reasoning it is meant to explain. He holds that 'ought' judgments are beliefs that can be true or false, but that an explanation is needed of how that can be so.

His basic idea, which is the main focus of the first part of this book, is that in believing that we ought to do a certain thing, we are really expressing our plans or our planning attitudes toward a certain course of action. The same is true of assessing the actions of others; it amounts to adopting a plan. Even to determine whether Caesar ought to have crossed the Rubicon when he did is to adopt a contingency plan for what to do if one is Caesar at the Rubicon then. All questions of what we or anyone else ought to do are planning questions; arriving at a conclusion about what ought to be done is really a matter of adopting a plan.

All three commentators challenge this identification, for different but related reasons. The objections would go to the heart of Gibbard's account of practical thought. Michael Bratman observes that the practical attitude we express in actually acting in a certain way cannot be the same as having adopted a plan to act in that way, since it is possible when the time comes to act contrary to what one even sincerely and resolutely plans to do. Gibbard sees in this objection the phenomenon sometimes called "weakness of will": doing something while remaining convinced at the very moment of action that one ought not to do it. Without denying the familiar facts of human action or inaction usually thought to illustrate it, Gibbard eventually wonders, with Plato's Socrates, whether there really is such a thing.

Frances Kamm defends the idea that there is something to be known or at least believed in practical reflection. Although she relies on "intuitive" judgments about particular cases in her own work in moral philosophy, she concedes that awareness or "intuitions" of what ought to be done are fallible and often need independent reasons and argument to support them. But she contends that in considering such reasons and assessing their force, even their force in favor of adopting a plan to act in certain ways, we evaluate considerations that hold or not independently of any plan we have adopted to rely on them. Gibbard does not exactly disagree, but for him finding certain reasons to be genuine and worth relying on is nothing more than coming to adopt a plan to trust them or rely on them.

John Broome objects that the attitudes of planning that Gibbard says are expressed in what look like beliefs about what ought to be done could never be identified or discovered in an agent without thinking of the person as already believing that such-and-such is best or ought to be done. The beliefs Gibbard sees as secondary or derivative from more basic planning attitudes must be taken as primary in recognizing the presence of the very attitudes said to be primary. Gibbard resists this idea on what for him is the fundamental ground from which he starts: that if such alleged 'ought' beliefs are not seen as planning attitudes along the lines he suggests, there can be no explanation of what they amount to, since there are no conditions in the world under which they would be true.

In the second and third lectures, Gibbard goes on to develop some of the consequences of the idea that the adoption of planning attitudes is what lies at the center of practical life. Planning is something that can be done alone. But people must also plan how to live together and, ideally, they must plan together how to live together. This kind of social coordination requires that one person's thoughts about what ought to be done must be taken into account in another person's thinking about what ought to be done. But each person seeks goals or goods that can apparently be understood and sought for independently of considerations of morality or of their contribution to general social harmony: happiness, accomplishment, human attachments, for instance. Gibbard thinks any planning one could enter into with others must offer the prospect to the planning agent of goods such as these. This would be what morality can be seen to be good for—how morality can serve mankind rather than having to be served by it.

The main question to which Gibbard's last two lectures are devoted is whether and how people's different aims or different conceptions of what is good can be acknowledged and accommodated within this kind of communal planning. It might seem that our living and acting together should not require that we all have a common set of goals or a single conception of the good. Any attempt to insist on such a single scheme or to impose it on all prospective agents could give some people reason not to plan to live that way. But Gibbard thinks planning that allows for such potential diversity of goods will prove to be unstable, even "incoherent"; it leaves room for the pursuit of goals that might conflict. He seeks a way of planning together that excludes this possibility but that each person could still see to be to his or her own good. To accept such a plan would be a way of honoring the idea of living with others in ways that one could justify to them, and so living together with others on terms of equal respect.

These apparently more 'contractual' considerations that must be present in any ideal plan for living together might seem incompatible with utilitarian forms of assessment that would evaluate outcomes only in terms of some overall good. But Gibbard argues that the kind of plan he sees as satisfying these 'contractual' requirements best is one the implementation of which would maximize the prospects of the total good of all participants. This is something he finds to be supported by two theorems in decision theory. John Broome questions Gibbard's use of the theorems he relies on. Can he really get from the theorems the results he wants? And does he really need the theorems in question to get the results he seeks? Gibbard's detailed response qualifies the original claim and more fully explains how he thinks it is to be defended.

This takes Gibbard in his replies into a detailed discussion of several different but closely related forms of contractual social theory. The question is whether and how their requirements can or cannot be accounted for on broadly utilitarian grounds. Frances Kamm raises many questions about the extent to which the version Gibbard proposes can respect basically 'contractual' requirements while assuring benefits to the participants that can be appreciated in fully nonmoral terms. The question whether a morality can be supported on extra-moral grounds is not definitively settled in these pages.

Gibbard's reply is in effect his defence of a plan that would be utilitarian in containing a common scale of goals or goods for all to pursue in which each person who accepts that scale and seeks those goals would advance the overall good as much as possible. Gibbard does not venture a suggestion as to what that scale of goals for all to pursue in common might be; it is a question of what is to count in a social contract that everyone can find reason to agree to. But he argues that on the general scheme he envisages, there must be such a thing as a person's good, since for anyone to accept a plan that would maximize the total good of everyone in this way would be to accept as the person's good whatever can be seen to play the relevant role in the plan the person accepts and lives by. What a person's good "really is" thereby also turns out to be a "planning question."

Both in the lectures and in his detailed replies to the challenging objections raised here, Allan Gibbard greatly extends his explanation and defence of the provocative position he has developed in recent decades. His contributions continue to reveal more and more of the sources, and of the power, of his distinctive approach to some of the most difficult problems of moral philosophy.

Reconciling Our Aims

ALLAN GIBBARD

I. Insight, Consistency, and Plans for Living

Jonathan Haidt, the social psychologist, entitles a fascinating article "The Emotional Dog and Its Rational Tail." His topic is moral judgment, and the emotional dog is what he calls "intuition." Mostly, he argues, we don't arrive at our moral conclusions by reasoning. We jump to them with emotional judgments, with "affectively valenced intuitions," as he puts it. We will often be firmly convinced that our moral judgments rest on sound reasoning, and that unless others are driven by bias, they will appreciate the force of our arguments. He calls this the "wag-the-other-dog's tail" illusion. In fact, though, in our moral reasoning, we are not so much like intuitive scientists following the considerations where they lead, but like intuitive lawyers, reasoning to preordained conclusions. Reasoning is effective on occasion, he concedes, with "adequate time and processing capacity, a motivation to be accurate, no a priori judgment to defend and justify, and when no relatedness or coherence motivations are triggered" (822). Mostly, though, what reasoning does is to construct "justifications of intuitive judgments, causing the illusion of objective reasoning" (822).[1]

All this chimes in with Hume's dictum, "Reason is, and ought only to be, the slave of the passions." Haidt himself isn't talking about how moral judgment *ought* to work; he is offering a psychological account of how moral judgment *does* work. Now even philosophers who stress reasoning have often thought that reasoning must rest ultimately on intuition. Intuitions give us the starting points of reasoning, and they tell us what follows immediately from what. Reasoning thus strings together a series of intuitions. Haidt's thesis isn't just that intuition is crucial to moral judgment, but that it isn't this stringing together that mostly drives moral judgment. Reasoning he defines as going by conscious steps, so that it "is intentional, effortful, and controllable and that the reasoner is aware that it is going on" (818). What's powerful in moral judgment, Haidt argues, will be the single, emotionally valenced intuition that reaches its conclusion all by itself. Moral judgment doesn't have to be this way, for all Hume's dictum tells us, but that, Haidt argues, is the way moral judgments mostly are.

We can ask whether what Haidt means by "intuition" is what philosophers have traditionally meant. The paradigm of intuition in the philosophical tradition has often been the geometric intuition by which we know the axioms of geometry. These are emotionally cool, whereas the intuitions that drive most moral judgment, according to Haidt, have emotions attached. It's an important question whether the intuitions that ground morality are always tied in with emotion, but that's not a question I'll be addressing. Later on I'll distinguish senses of the term 'intuition,' but I won't restrict the term either to "hot" or to "cool" states of mind.

Now, we philosophers aren't expert psychologists. It's how we *ought* to reason that we are specially charged with assessing. Often we do reason, even on moral questions, and I'll assume that sometimes we should. The philosopher's job in particular is to reason, and if we ought never to reason on morals, then we moral philosophers may need to find another line of work. In this lecture, though, I won't engage in moral reasoning; that is for the next two lectures. My questions in this lecture will be *about* moral reasoning. What is its subject matter? I'll ask. How ought we to reason? If reasoning strings together intuitions, why trust its intuitive starting points? I'll talk about these broad questions in this lecture, and then in the next two scrutinize a particular piece of moral reasoning, one that purports to get remarkably strong moral conclusions from plain and clear intuitions.

Moral intuitions are puzzling. We seem to have moral knowledge; indeed some moral truths seem so utterly clear as to be pointless to state. It's wrong to torture people for fun. Other moral questions are agonizing to ponder. Are there any conceivable circumstances in which we would be morally justified in torturing someone? If we have moral knowledge at all, it seems this knowledge must rest in the end on powers to intuit moral truths. G. E. Moore a hundred years ago elaborated arguments that moral claims aren't claims that could be brought within the purview of natural science. Two people could agree on all the facts of empirical science and still disagree morally. They could disagree, say, on whether, as Henry Sidgwick thought, pleasure is the only thing worth wanting for its own sake. The fault of the one who is wrong needn't rest on ignorance of the facts of nature, or failure to grasp the concepts involved, or any failure of logic.[2] Natural facts and conceptual truths aren't enough to entail answers to moral questions. If we are to have any moral knowledge at all, then, the gap must somehow be filled. What else could it be filled by but a power of intuition, a power to apprehend some basic moral truths, though not by the senses?[3]

Not all philosophers agree that morality lies outside the scope of empirical science, but I'll be offering a picture on which it does, and proceed on the assumption that the picture is right. Moreover, I would argue that even claims about rationality in science aren't entirely within the subject matter of science. Science itself rests on intuitions about the justification of empirical conclusions. If that's right, then it may not only be morality that raises puzzles about intuition.

In the case of morality in particular, a chief puzzle is, it is hard to see how beings like us could have powers of moral intuition. We are parts of the natural world. Crucial aspects of any moral truth, though, don't lie in the natural world. When we look at ourselves as parts of the natural world—as Haidt does—we won't find a responsiveness to anything non-natural. We won't even find the purported facts we claim to intuit.

I'll begin what I have to say by sketching a view of ourselves as a part of nature. Moral right and wrong form no part of this view. It is part of the view, though, that we would ask ourselves moral questions and come to conclusions about them. How things stand morally is not a part of the natural world, but our study of these matters is. (Later I'll be qualifying this, but for now let's stick with it.) Beings who think and reason about what to do, I say, answer questions of ought, at least implicitly, when they settle on what to do. Beings with our own psychic makeup make specifically moral claims. I'll speculate how these activities look within a value-free scientific picture. After that, I'll turn to the plight of the beings like us who figure in the picture, beings who think about what to do and think about right and wrong. Our answers to the questions we address will rest on intuitions—but, I'll be asking, if intuitions are the sorts of states that figure in Haidt's picture, why place any stock in them?[4]

Nature, Oughts, and Plans

Begin, then, with us as living organisms who are part of the world of living organisms. The upshot of natural selection is that genes become amazingly good at, as it were, working together to use us to make more copies of themselves. How, a great puzzle runs, have metaphorically selfish genes come to make people who are, literally, not entirely selfish? The answer can only be a long and controversial story, and I won't address this particular story in these lectures. Rather, I'll ask about the place of *oughts* in the story, in this world of *is*s.

The story proceeds in terms of the metaphorical interests of the genes, the things that promoted their multiplying as the human genotype was formed, and on the other hand, the literal aims, beliefs, and feelings of humans and proto-humans. Genes proliferate in part by forming recipes for organisms that keep track of the world around them, very much including the social world.[5] Knowledge guides action. But it guides action in ways that proliferate genes only if the actors have the right aims, the right propensities to use their knowledge to guide action. Knowing where a lion is doesn't promote one's genes' reproduction if one's reaction is to try to pet it.

The beings in this biological picture of us, then, face questions of how things are, but those aren't the primary questions they face. The primary questions are ones of what to do, what to aim for and how. Most organisms of course can't be interpreted, in any full-bodied sense, as addressing these questions and accepting or rejecting answers to them. Dogs chase squirrels and bark at intruders, and much of the time, we, like the dog, just act out of habit or emotion. We, though, of an intricately social species with language, differ from other animals in two important ways. First, our social emotions are especially refined and elaborate. A substantial amount of the human neo-cortex seems to function in the workings of emotions, and emotions include impulses to action. Many of our feelings are intensely social, as with guilt and resentment, with shame and disdain. Second, we are beings with language, and we make judgments that we express with language.

Here, then, are two pieces of speculation about our species. First, we are adapted to specific kinds of emotional reactions to social situations. These reactions include moral emotions of resentment or outrage and of guilt, guided by judgments of fairness. Emotions bring characteristic tendencies to action, so that resentment, for instance, tends toward punitive action. Emotions thus affect reproduction through the actions they prompt, and so natural selection will shape the psychic mechanisms of emotion. Human emotional proclivities evolved the way they did because of this. With humans also, though, I speculate, there evolved a kind of language-infused governance of emotions. We discuss together and have linguistically encoded thoughts that work to control our feelings. On feeling a flash of resentment that you took a piece of cake that I had hoped to have, I can reason that you were as much within your rights to take it as I would have been, and so there is no cause for resentment. At this thought, my resentment may subside. If it doesn't and I complain, expressing my resentment, the rest of you may set me straight. If my resentment doesn't subside, the actions it prompts may, in my social circumstances, work in the long run to hurt my reproductive prospects. Hence come selection pressures for a genetic propensity to control emotions in certain sorts of social circumstances.

My resentment is unwarranted, I judge, when you finish the cake. How does a concept like warrant work? For purposes of delineating how reasoning with such concepts can go, I suggest we think of judgments of warrant as something like plans. I plan, as it were, under what circumstances to resent people for things they do. This talk of plans for feelings sounds artificial, I admit, but when we judge that resentment would be unwarranted in my situation, the judgment acts much as would a plan, for my situation, not to resent you. Literal plans are carried out by choice, to be sure, and we can't choose what to feel. Feelings, though, do respond somewhat to judgments of warrant, as they might in the example. It's thus somewhat as if we planned what to feel, even though choice doesn't figure in the guidance of emotion in the way that plans for action get realized by guiding choice.[6]

Questions of moral right and wrong, on this picture, will be questions of what to do, but with a particular kind of emotional flavor. What is it to think an act morally wrong, as opposed to just silly or imprudent? Roughly, I propose, it is to think that the act warrants resentment on the part of others and guilt on the part of the person who did it. Specifically moral questions, if this is right, are questions of what moral sentiments to have toward things. At their narrowest, they are questions of what to resent people for doing and what to feel guilty for doing. To guilt and resentment here, as Howard Nye has urged on me, we need to add a prospective feeling of guilt-tinged aversion toward acts we might contemplate doing.[7] This emotion is negatively valenced toward the act, and so to plan guilt-tinged aversion toward an act is to plan to be against one's doing it, in a way that has a particular emotional flavor. (Whether planning this aversion must always go with planning, all things considered, not to do the act is an important question that I won't try to answer here.)

I am contrasting, then, oughts in general and moral oughts. Narrowly moral questions of right and wrong I'm treating as at base questions of what moral sentiments we ought to have and act from. Questions in the broader class of oughts in general we call *normative* questions. These include questions of what a person ought to do all things considered. They include epistemological questions of what we ought to believe. And they include questions of how we ought to feel about things. These, I am saying, are all, in a broad, extended sense, planning questions; they are questions of what to do, to think, and to feel. Moral questions are planning questions of a particular kind, questions of how to feel about things, where the feelings in question are the moral sentiments.

Explaining Oughts

A dictum that we draw from Hume is that you can't derive an *ought* purely from an *is*, and G. E. Moore argued that oughts don't form a part of the natural world that empirical science can study. The picture I have sketched has the upshot that Moore was right. The scientific picture tells us why organisms like us would have questions whose answers can't be made a part of science. The point is that not only do we think about how things are, but we also act and feel. Our actions and feelings figure in a biological account, along with the goings-on in the head that lead to actions and to feelings about things. Questions of what to do and why, and questions of how to feel about things and why, won't figure in the picture. Yet the picture shows us addressing those questions.

Suppose I settle on helping a man in need even though I won't get any advantage from it. I think I ought to help him, and that it would be wrong not to do so, and so I help him. My coming to these conclusions must be part of any full and adequate naturalistic, biological story of me. The story, though, won't contain any fact that I've got my conclusions right or not. It doesn't contain a fact that I ought to help or that it's okay not to. It doesn't contain a fact that it would be wrong not to help or that it wouldn't be. Questions of what I ought to do and what it would be wrong to do or not to do aren't questions amenable to science. They are, I have been saying, questions of whether to help and of how to feel about not helping. A scientific picture, then, has us asking questions that don't have scientific answers. The picture shows too why these questions aren't luxuries, but must be central questions for us. And from the scientific picture comes an account of what these questions are: They are questions of what to do and how to feel about things people do or might do. If these are the questions, we don't need to worry that they concern queer goings-on that form no part of the fabric of the universe, as John Mackie puts it.[8] They are intelligible questions, and they are questions of first importance.

I have been contrasting questions of empirical science and questions of what to do and how to feel. I should note, though, that this may not get matters quite right. Perhaps the two-way split I have made really ought to be a three-way split. First, as I've been saying, there's the empirical picture of us as special parts of the natural world, shaped as a species, as it were, by natural selection, and shaped as individuals in society by complex social dynamics, a complex human ecology. The empirical sciences of psychology, sociology, anthropology, and the like all contribute to this. Next, though, there's a part I haven't singled out: interpretation. We understand some of these natural goings-on as beliefs, assertions, plans, and the like with which we can agree or disagree. The ought part then comes third in the list, as we seek answers to the questions we can be interpreted as asking. So we have three areas of inquiry:

psycho-social science, interpretation, and normative inquiry. When I speak of a person as thinking that she ought to help, and when I say that this amounts to deciding to help, I'm interpreting certain goings-on in her as the having of these thoughts.

As a first approximation, then, I'm saying, *ought* thoughts are like plans. Thinking what I ought to do amounts to thinking what to do. But this dictum needs refining. Thinking what to do can go in two stages: In the first stage, I form my valences or preferences. In the second stage, if there's more than one thing I equally and most prefer from among my alternatives, I pick one—not out of preference, but out of the necessity to choose if I'm not to be like Buridan's ass. My strictly normative thinking is a matter of the first stage. We could call this part concluding what's "okay" to do and what isn't. When it's okay to do something and not okay not to, then I *ought* to do it. Thinking what I ought to do, then, is not all of thinking what to do. Rather, it's the part that matters, the valenced stage.

This ties in with a worry about the right direction of explanation. It may well be objected that I have the proper direction of explanation reversed. I started out explaining *ought* beliefs as plans. But this, even if it is right, doesn't explain normative belief in general. It doesn't explain belief in ties for what it would be best to do, the belief that more than one alternative would be okay. The belief that something is rationally okay to do, then, has to be explained in some other way—and once we have this explanation, it's easy to explain the concept ought. That a person *ought* to do a thing just means that it's okay to do it and not okay not to do it. Since we can't explain an *okay* in terms of plans, perhaps we are forced to become normative realists. We start by establishing that being okay to do is a property we can know some acts to have, and then go on from there to explain the concept *ought* and what plans consist in. That is the objection: I have tried to explain the concept *ought* in terms of plans, but the explanation, it turns out, can only run in the other direction. I answer that we can explain both concepts, *okay* and *ought,* in terms of something we do on the way to planning: forming valences. The explanation is oblique: I don't offer straight definitions of the terms 'okay' and 'ought' in terms of planning. Rather, I say what *believing* an act to be okay consists in. To believe it okay is to rule out preferring any alternative. It is thus to rule out a kind of valence. Normative judgments, we can say, consist in valences and restrictions on valences.

This, I'm claiming, explains the philosophically puzzling notions of what one *ought* to do and what it's *okay* to do. It explains the "to be doneness" that John Mackie thought to be no part of the fabric of the universe. It explains how G. E. Moore and other non-naturalists could argue so convincingly that ethical thought deals with non-natural properties. Many philosophers think that the right direction of explanation is the opposite. An answer to the question of how to live, they would say, just is a belief as to what we ought to do and what it's at least okay to do. Now of course anyone who says this has the burden of explaining what 'ought' and 'okay' mean. If they can't, or if their answer involves strange and incredible things like non-natural properties, I then say that my direction of explanation is better. I start my explanation with something intelligible, with decision and the valences and restrictions that get a person to the final stage where, if need be, he goes from indifference to picking something.

Intuitions

Return now to the subject I started out with, to moral intuition. I am treating moral inquiry as inquiry into how to live and how to feel, how to engage people and their actions emotionally. Often, though, moral inquiry is conducted by consulting moral "intuitions"—and indeed Sidgwick, Ross, and others have argued that moral reasoning couldn't get off the ground without moral intuitions. This alleged power of moral intuition Mackie attacked as incredible, as a purported mode of knowledge that is unlike any other we know.[9] How could we be in any position to intuit moral truths, or normative truths in general? No answer is apparent in the biological picture I sketched. Non-natural facts are absent from the picture, and so are any powers to get at non-natural truths by intuition. Interpreting the natural goings-on as thoughts and judgments doesn't change this. If moral knowledge must depend on intuition, we seem driven to moral skepticism.

Intuitions would give knowledge, perhaps, if we had a kind of inner eye that peers into the non-natural layout of moral facts—but that's not a picture to take seriously. Another stance we can take toward intuition is not to worry: We rely on intuition, after all, for mathematical knowledge, and so why should morality be more constrained in the ways we can know it? Now the question of how we have mathematical knowledge is difficult. Still, at least for arithmetic and geometry, mathematics is part and parcel of empirical knowledge, the knowledge we get by counting, measuring, and the like. Our abilities to get numbers right are aspects of our abilities to get right such empirical matters as the number of pebbles in a basket. If our abilities to get morality right were like this, there wouldn't be the same puzzle about them. There would be difficult philosophical explaining to do, as with our knowledge of arithmetic and geometry, but there would be no sheer mystery as to why evolved beings like us would have powers of veridical insight in the realm of morality.

Another possibility would be that intuitions matter because the moral question just is what our moral convictions would be in reflective equilibrium, when we had given adequate heed to everything that would affect our considered moral beliefs. Moral intuitions would matter, then, as the starting points for reaching reflective equilibrium. I'm claiming, though, that moral claims aren't claims in interpreted psychology. The question of what we would think if such-and-such conditions obtained is mostly an empirical one, along with the further question of how to interpret the state we would then be in. I have been saying that the moral question isn't what we *would* think in such-and-such conditions, but what to do and how to feel about things we do or might do. These questions aren't answered by interpreted psychology alone.

Now it might seem that I have escaped the problem of relying on intuitions. If normative thoughts are plans, or valenced restrictions on plans, then to come to normative conclusions, we just have to plan. This, however, doesn't free us from intuitions. As we plan, we'll weigh considerations for and against actions. Take even a case of non-moral planning, thinking whether to go to the store. In favor I might weigh the consideration that there I can get cigarettes. I can go on to evaluate whether to weigh that consideration in favor. I settle what to weigh into my decision and how, and form a string of considerations that support other considerations. At some point, though, the string comes to an end. Perhaps I weigh the fact that I'd enjoy smoking in favor of smoking, on no further ground. And perhaps I weigh the chance that I'd suffer if I smoked against a plan to smoke. Weighing enjoyment in favor and suffering against, on no further ground, amounts to having an intuition about why to do things. Intuitions, then, apply to planning, and not just to thinking how things stand. If I keep challenging my thoughts about what to do and why, I end up grounding my planning in intuition.

I accept, then, that normative thinking rests on intuition. This seems to raise the same question again: Why think we can intuit why to do things? Like questions go for thinking how to feel and why: why think we can intuit why and why not to feel certain ways about things? But thinking of ought judgments as plans leads to an answer. I intuit, we said, that the chance that I'd suffer if I did a thing is reason not to do it. But to say that I have this intuition is just another way of saying that I confidently weigh the chance of suffering against doing a thing, and on no further ground even if I ask myself why.

To say this is to use the term 'intuition' in an empirical, non-normative sense, as Haidt does—as a certain kind of state of mind that is open to empirical study. We could instead use the term, though, in a normative sense: An intuition, we could say, is a state of mind of accepting something, not on the basis of further reasoning even upon challenge, that we ought to place some trust in. To think something an intuition in this sense is to plan to rely on it. I'll call intuitions in the non-normative sense in which they figure in psychology "de facto" intuitions. These are judgments made confidently, on no further grounds, with no felt need for further grounds even upon challenge. Intuitions in the normative sense I'll call intuitions "de jure." These are de facto intuitions to rely on. It's a normative claim, then, that de facto intuitions are genuine intuitions—and one we need, I have been claiming, for coherent planning.

Ideal Conditions

I have been stressing the distinction between non-normative psychological questions of how we do form moral judgments and normative questions of how we ought to. What we will plan under what conditions is a psychological question, whereas normative questions are planning questions of what to do. The two are closely tied to each other, though. We can ask the planning question of when to trust our own planning. We can ask under what conditions to trust our planning most. That amounts to asking what conditions are ideal for planning. Ideal conditions, we might conclude, involve such things as full information vividly taken in and contemplated, and an alert, engaged, and dispassionate frame of mind. If we come to a precise view about what those conditions are, we can then ask the psychological question of what, in those conditions, we would plan.

I face a moral dilemma, suppose—I'll give as an example a simple and far-fetched dilemma that I'll talk more about tomorrow. A father stands on the bank of a river where two canoes have capsized with children in them. His own daughter was in the far canoe, and he can rescue her. Alternatively, though, he could rescue two children of strangers who are nearer to him. He can't do both; what ought he to do?

This first is an ought question; now we can ask another kind of question: How would we answer this first question in ideal conditions for judgment? If we get an answer to the second, psychological question, we'll come to an answer to the first. Suppose I conclude, "Under ideal conditions for judgment, I'd judge that he ought to rescue his daughter, even though that means rescuing only one child when he could have rescued two." Relying on myself as I'd judge in ideal conditions, I can now say, "He ought to rescue his daughter instead of the other two children."

It's not that the moral conclusion is *entailed* by a finding in interpreted psychology. Rather, what's going on is this: When we call conditions for judgment "ideal," we mean that judgments in those conditions are ones to trust. To accept this is to plan to trust such judgments. So I accept the claim, imagine,

> In ideal conditions, I would judge that the man ought to rescue his daughter.

Equivalently, I accept this:

> The judgment that he ought to rescue his daughter is one to trust.

To accept this is to plan to trust this judgment, the judgment that the man ought to rescue his daughter. To trust the judgment means being disposed to emulate it in one's own judgment. So following through on the plan, I make the judgment,

> The man ought to rescue his daughter.

If, then, we could settle under what conditions to trust our normative judgments, then we could come to normative conclusions on the basis of interpreted empirical findings. From the empirical finding that in those conditions for contemplation I'd judge the man ought to rescue his daughter, I could reason to judging that he ought to rescue his daughter and voice my state of mind by saying that he ought to rescue his daughter. This isn't deriving an *ought* from a psychological *is* alone, for there's an intervening normative premise. The premise amounts to this: that what I'd *find* wrong in those particular conditions *is* wrong—that what I would then *think* ought to be done *ought* to be done.

Possibly, then, we could find a systematic way to move from psychological findings to moral conclusions. In many kinds of cases, after all, a transition from *is* to *ought* is entirely obvious and uncontroversial. If you're driving late to work and a child will be killed unless you stop, then you ought to stop. How to weigh a child's life against arriving promptly at work is something we've settled beyond need for further review. If the conditions under which to trust one's normative judgments were similarly unproblematic, then the problematic parts of ethics would be reduced to questions of interpreted psychology. The move from *is* to *ought* still wouldn't be one of entailment, but it might be systematic and trustworthy. We aren't at that point yet, though—and if we did get there, it would still be important to distinguish *ought* questions from psychological questions, to keep track of what we had achieved and what our basis was for accepting the ought conclusions we accepted.

Coherence and Inconsistency

Plans, I claimed, require intuitions, but I need to make this claim more precisely. At a moment, I can find it clear that the fact that I'd enjoy something weighs in favor of doing it. I can then rely on this as a premise without relying on the further psychological premise that I find this obvious. No thoughts about intuition enter into my thinking, and I haven't skipped over any steps that would be needed to make my thinking explicit and fully cogent. Over time, though,

I can plan what to do only if, at least implicitly, I do place some stock in my earlier conclusions without rethinking them. I trust my earlier conclusions, and I can't be justified in doing this unless the fact that I earlier found something obvious on no further ground is at least some reason to accept it. Planning requires thinking that the *is* of interpreted psychology—that I implicitly accept an ought, and would accept it explicitly if challenged, on no further ground— supports accepting the *ought*. I must not only have de facto intuitions, but I must trust them; I must treat them as intuitions de jure.

I don't mean, though, that de facto intuitions are to be trusted entirely. Seeming intuitions can clash, and indeed seeming intuitions about what to do can clash severely. The trust to put in them can only be defeasible. Even if moral claims didn't mean what I say they do, and even if the visual model held good for intuitions of moral right and wrong, we'd have to test intuitions against each other and revise them in light of conflicts. Philosophical work on normative ethics, much of it, consists in engaging in this refinement of intuitions—but there's no end of controversy as to where the weight of corrected intuition falls.

I have been suggesting that we might get further by conceiving of our questions as ones of what to do and how to feel about things and why. This won't end our dependence on intuitions, but we can see if the intuitions we now rely on are more tractable. Much of what I'll be doing in the next lecture will go over ground familiar to moral philosophers, and we'll have to hope that the resulting treatment makes contact with ordinary moral thought, or there would be little reason to trust it. A lot of what I'll be saying in the next two lectures stems from decision theory and from arguments that decision theorists have made. We can think of decision theory as a systematic development of intuitions about what to do and why.

Decision theorists in the classical Bayesian tradition work to formulate what it means to be consistent in one's policies for action, and then derive surprisingly strong results from the conditions they lay down. This tradition stems from the work of, among others, L. J. Savage, who rediscovered a way of thinking that had been developed by F. P. Ramsey toward the end of his short life.[10] If a way of making choices satisfies the Savage conditions (or conditions in a like vein), as it turns out, then it is as if one were maximizing an expectation of value. It is as if, that is to say, one had numerical degrees of credence and numerical evaluations of the possible outcomes, and acted to maximize expected value as reckoned in terms of these evaluations and degrees of credence. (The term 'expected value' doesn't here mean what it would mean in ordinary English; one acts as if to maximize an expectation in the mathematical sense, summing up one's evaluations of the possible outcomes each weighted by one's degree of credence that it would be the outcome.) Bentham the hedonist was right at least formally, it seems to follow: If one's policies for action are consistent, one acts, in the face of uncertainty, to advance the good on some scale of evaluation. The scale may not gauge pleasure, but there will be some such scale or other.

The conditions that classical decision theorists put forth as innocuous and compelling, though, combine in ways that clash with strong intuitions. They are for that reason controversial; critics look to show that not all the classical conditions are genuinely demands of reason. In the lectures to come I rely heavily on the findings of classical decision theory, and so although I won't scrutinize the controversies in any depth, I'll glance at one famous example, due to Richard Zeckhauser.[11]

You are forced to play Russian roulette, but you can buy your way out. What is the most you would be willing to pay, the question is, to remove the bullet, reducing your chance of shooting yourself from one in six to zero. Or that's the first question; once you answer it, we ask a more complex one. You are instead, it turns out, forced to play a worse version of Russian roulette, with four bullets in the six chambers. What's the most you would pay, the question now is, to remove *one* of the four bullets. In particular, is it more or less than before?

Most people answer less. But you should pay *more*, goes an argument from orthodox decision theory. This problem is equivalent, after all, to a two-stage problem, as follows: In the first stage, you are forced to play with three bullets and no chance to buy yourself out. In the second stage, if you survive, you are forced to play with two bullets, but you can pay to remove both. The amount to pay in the second case, then, is anything you would pay to remove both of two bullets if they were the only two bullets—surely more than to remove one sole bullet.

This case and others like it have been staples of debate on the foundations of decision theory, and ways out of this conflict of intuitions have been proposed. The first thing to note, though, is that the intuitions in conflict are strong. Is removing two bullets worth more than removing one, if in each case you thereby empty the pistol? Surely. Does anything matter, in these choices, but the chance of surviving and how poor you will be if you do? Not much; those seem the predominant considerations. It doesn't matter, then, whether you must play the four-bullet game or the two-stage game, since they involve choice among the same chances of death. Does it matter if you choose at the start of the two-stage game what to pay if you survive the first stage, or decide once it turns out you have survived the first stage? Clearly not. Orthodox decision theory goes against intuition for this case, but any alternative to orthodoxy will violate one of the strong intuitions I just voiced. The constraints in classical decision theory that do the real work are all exemplified in the argument I just gave, and so at least for cases like this one, if the argument is good, then classical decision theory is pretty well vindicated.

I myself am convinced that what we gain in intuitiveness when we depart from the orthodox views in decision theory in cases like this is less than what we lose. That would be a long argument, though, and I can't expect you to accept this conclusion on my say-so. What I hope you are convinced of is that some of our strong intuitions will have to go whatever we hypothetically decide to do in the Zeckhauser case. In the lectures that follow, I'll proceed as if the conclusions of orthodox decision theory are right—but you should note that part of the argument remains to be discharged, and it is controversial among the experts whether it can be.[12]

I'll be assuming without further argument, then, that the constraints of decision theory are ones of consistency in action, or something close to it. Whether they are full-fledged matters of consistency is a tricky question, and so I'll use the word coherence. Why, though, does coherence in plans for action matter—especially when they are plans for wild contingencies that we will never face, like being forced to play any of several versions of Russian roulette? With questions of fact, the problem with inconsistency is that when a set of beliefs is inconsistent, at least one of the beliefs is false. I'm suggesting that we think of ought questions, in the first instance, as planning questions. Answers to them may in the end count as true or false, but we don't start our treatment with talk of truth and falsehood and help ourselves to these notions in our initial theorizing. With incoherent plans, I accept, the oughts we accept in having those plans can't all be true, but that isn't at the root of what's wrong. So, indeed, what *is* wrong with incoherent plans?

As a first approximation, I can say, incoherent plans can't all be carried out. If I plan to be here today and also plan to be on top of Mt. Kenya, believing that I can't be both places on the same day, my beliefs and plans are inconsistent. Either, then, my belief that I can't be in both places is false, or one of my plans I won't carry out no matter what choices I make. Some of the plans I'll be talking about tomorrow, though, are wild contingency plans that I'll never be in a position to carry out anyway. I might talk about such wild plans as for what to prefer for the contingency of being Brutus on the Ides of March. And some of the states of mind that can be coherent or not with others won't be simple plans but constraints on plans and beliefs—that, for instance, I plan to pay more, if forced to play Russian roulette, to empty the pistol of two bullets than of one.

The problem with inconsistent plans is that there is no way they can be realized in a complete contingency plan for living. For each full contingency plan one might have, something in the set will rule it out. Or more completely, we'd have to talk about inconsistent beliefs, plans, and constraints. If a set of these is inconsistent, there's no combination of a full contingency plan for living and a full way that world might be that fits. And judgments get their content from what they are consistent with and what not.

Preview

Today I have contrasted biological thinking about us and the normative thinking that the biological picture has us engaging in. A rich enough biological picture, I think, explains why a highly social, linguistic species like ours would engage in normative thinking and discussion, and in moral thinking and discussion in particular. I also talked about intuitions. We couldn't coherently proceed with normative thinking without giving some trust to some of our de facto intuitions, treating them as intuitions de jure. (Indeed I would claim that this applies to thinking of all kinds—but I haven't gone into that in this lecture.) At the same time, some of our strong intuitions are inconsistent with each other, and so our trust in de facto intuitions, to be coherent, must be guarded.

In the lectures that follow, I'll take this very high-level normative thinking about intuitions and reasoning and turn to morality. Our lives are social, and a large part of thinking what to do and how to feel is thinking how to live with other people. We address these questions partly each by ourselves and partly together in discussion. I'll be keeping my eye on moral thinking as thinking how to live with each other and on the question of how to regard our moral intuitions. The moral argument that I pursue and scrutinize is one that may be very powerful, but that raises difficult questions. This is an argument that owes the most to Berkeley's late John Harsanyi. It leads to conclusions that clash with strong moral intuitions, and I'll be trying to think through the force of these intuitions. In the two lectures that follow, then, instead of just describing moral thinking as thinking how to live with each other, I'll engage in moral thinking in a reflective and highly theoretical way.

Notes

1. Haidt, "The Emotional Dog and Its Rational Tail" (2001).
2. Moore, *Principia Ethica* (1903). The argument of Moore's that I find powerful is the one on p. 11 that I call his "What's at issue?" argument.
3. Sidgwick, *Methods of Ethics* (1907), pp. 338–42, argues that ethics requires at least one intuition.
4. The picture I develop is given in my books *Wise Choices, Apt Feelings* (1990) and *Thinking How to Live* (2003). For a discussion centered on intuition, see my "Knowing What to Do" (2002), and for second thoughts on the theory of moral concepts in *Wise Choices,* see my "Moral Feelings" (2006).
5. My talk of "recipes" is drawn from Marcus, "Birth of the Mind" (2004), a treatment of how genetic recipes lead to phenotypes.
6. In "Reply" (2006) I address objections to this talk of "plans" as part of a symposium with Simon Blackburn and Neil Sinclair, Michael Bratman, Jamie Dreier, and T. M. Scanlon.
7. Personal communications and unpublished papers.
8. Mackie, *Ethics* (1977).
9. Mackie, *Ethics* (1977). On the necessity for intuitions, see Sidgwick, *Methods of Ethics* (1907), and Ross, *The Right and the Good* (1930), esp. pp. 39–41.
10. Classic developments of decision-theoretic arguments are Ramsey, "Truth and Probability" (1931), and Savage, *Foundations of Probability* (1957). Hammond, "Consequentialist Foundations"

(1988), develops a framework in terms of sequential decisions, and this offers, I think, the clearest case that departing from the strictures of classical decision theory is incoherent. Unfortunately, Hammond's argument is couched in fearsome mathematical apparatus.

11. The example is presented in Kahneman and Tversky, "Prospect Theory" (1979), p. 283. It is a version of the famous "Allais paradox" for classical decision theory.

12. For critiques of classical decision theory with references, see, for instance, Sen, "Rationality and Uncertainty" (1985), and McClennen, *Rationality and Dynamic Choice* (Cambridge University Press, 1990).

II. Living Together: Economic and Moral Argument

We are beings who think about how to live. We live each with others, and we think how to live with each other. Sometimes we think about such things each by ourselves, and sometimes we think and discuss together. These are truisms, but I argued in the first lecture that the truisms are rich in consequences. They explain, if I am right, the philosophically puzzling area of thought we call "normative," thought that somehow involves oughts.

I want to ask in this lecture and the next whether such a self-understanding could have any bearing on questions of right and wrong, of good and bad. In the first lecture I talked about moral concepts without using them. I did metaethics, not normative ethics, not the work of thinking through what *is* right and what *is* wrong and why. My metaethics leaves room for any coherent answer whatever to normative questions of what's right and what's wrong to do—and a wide range of possible answers are coherent. I want, though, to explore whether the metaethical picture I sketched contributes at all to making some answers to normative questions more plausible than others. In doing so, I'll have to pass lightly over controversies familiar in the literature of ethical theory, giving quick and insufficient arguments on issues that have been extensively and subtly debated.

A Social Contract and the Strains of Commitment

My late colleague William Frankena finished his short book *Ethics* with the dictum, "Morality is made for man, not man for morality."[1] His saying is widely quoted. He told me that he regretted ever saying this, but I don't see that he had anything to regret. If morality should matter to us, if we should adhere to moral demands even at great sacrifice, then morality shouldn't be arbitrary. Concern for morality should be out of concern for something that makes morality of value—and how could that thing be anything other than being of value for people? (I don't mean to rule out other sentient beings, but in these lectures I'll stick to people.)

Most philosophers, I think, will agree with Frankena's saying, but we fall into contention when it comes to drawing out its implications. Moral inquiry in philosophy often comes in either of two broad styles. One is humanistic and pragmatic, thinking what's in morality for us, for us human beings, and asking what version of morality best serves us. The other broad style is intuitionist, in one important sense of that term: Consult our moral intuitions, revise them as need be to achieve consistency, and embrace what emerges. The point isn't that these two styles of moral inquiry need entirely be at odds with each other. The hope in consulting and systematizing intuitions is that doing so will uncover a deep, implicit rationale for our intuitive responses, and that the rationale we discover will turn out to be a worthy one. The hope is thus that, carried out in the right way, the two broad styles converge. Humanistic pragmatists start out with a vague rationale for ethics, a value ethics has that can be appreciated in non-ethical terms. As Henry Sidgwick argued over a century ago, however, a morality made for humanity must in the end be grounded on some intuition—an intuition, perhaps, as to how humanity matters.[2] His vision was, then, that the two approaches, pragmatic and intuitive, amount to the same approach. Still, initially at least, the two are quite different in spirit.

If morality is for humanity, then we might expect utilitarianism to be right. Moral rules, we might expect, will tell us each to act for the benefit of all humanity. The right act will be the one with the greatest total benefit to people. Utilitarianism, though, notoriously conflicts with strong moral intuitions. As a simple example, I'll start with the case from yesterday of children drowning. I'll then broach a line of argument that appeals to other intuitions and seems to lead back to the utilitarian answer. The case illustrates a much broader, systematic argument for utilitarianism, one that draws on decision theory and was most notably advanced by Berkeley's own John Harsanyi well before he came to Berkeley. Aspects of the argument have been widely debated, and my aim is to use the debate to explore how moral inquiry might proceed if it consists in doing the sort of thing I claim, in thinking how to live together.

The case is due to Diane Jeske and Richard Fumerton.[3] Two canoes of children capsize in rapids, and a man on the bank can rescue some but not all of the children. Close to him are two children, and he could rescue both. Further away is his own daughter, and alternatively he could rescue her but not the other two. Utilitarianism seems to say that, faced with this grim choice, he should rescue the two children rather than the one. Many people have the strong intuition that the father is morally permitted—perhaps even required by the duties of parenthood—to rescue his daughter, even though he must then let two children drown instead of one.

This example is contrived, in the style of many philosophical examples. The hope is, though, that such examples can let us examine considerations in isolation that get too complex to handle clearly in the kinds of morally fraught situations we are most apt to encounter.

I'll now introduce the style of argument that I'll be exploring. Imagine now that the situation is a little more complex. There are two fathers on the two river banks by the rapids, and two canoes are swamped, each with two children. For each father, his own children are in the farther canoe. Each could save either the two children closest to him, or one but not both of his own children in the far canoe. The rule to give preference to one's own children, if each father follows it, means that each father loses a child. The rule to save as many children as possible, regardless of whose they are, means, if each father follows it, that no father loses a child.

Perhaps in this freak circumstance, the two fathers could quickly reach an agreement that each would rescue the other's children. They would then each have a contractual obligation to act as utilitarianism would command, and for this case, the contrast between intuition and utilitarianism might disappear. In its prescriptions for this particular case, a social contract would thus coincide with utilitarianism.

Return, though, to the first story, with one father whose child was in the far, swamped canoe. Suppose that in advance, the two fathers contemplate this contingency. One of them will be on the bank, with one of his two children swamped in the far canoe. Both children of the other will be in the near canoe. The man on the bank will be able, then, to save either both of the other father's children or one of his own. The fathers might come to a social contract covering this eventuality. What would it be? Suppose first that they agree that each is to save his own in preference to saving both the nearer children. If they know the agreement will be kept, then each stands to lose both of his children if he's the unlucky father who has two children at risk and can't rescue either one, and to lose no child in case he's there to do the rescuing. Next, suppose instead they agree that each will rescue as many children as he can. Then if the agreement will be kept, each stands to lose one child if he's the unlucky father on the bank, acting on his agreement, and to lose no child if he's the lucky absent father whose children get rescued by the other. In short, then, so long as whatever agreement they reach they will keep, then the first agreement in the unlucky case means losing both one's children, whereas the second in the unlucky case means losing only one child. Each is a terrible loss, but losing both children is even worse than losing one—and the two cases are equally likely, we have supposed. For each father, then, the second agreement offers the better prospect.

Again, then, for the case in question, two approaches give the same answer. Utilitarianism says to rescue as many children as one can, and so does the social contract that people would make if they knew that the social contract would be kept.

This kind of argument generalizes. John Harsanyi in the 1950s proved two famous theorems that apply—theorems which I think should be more famous than they are among students of moral philosophy. The import and the limitations of his theorems have been debated in the philosophical and economic literature, and I'll be exploring how some aspects of the discussion might go if moral inquiry is the sort of thing I think it is: planning how to live with each other.

First, though, let's explore further the case of the children and the swamped canoes. The two fathers have agreed what to do in the contingency, and now one of them finds himself in the dilemma on the river bank. He has agreed to save the two children that aren't his, but still, of course, he is strongly moved to save his own child. What motive might he have to keep the agreement and let his own child drown? His motive might be one of fair reciprocity. "He would have done the same for my two children if our positions had been reversed," he can say to himself. Still, he faces the question of whether to reciprocate. Possibly, fair reciprocity will insufficiently motivate him, and he will fail to reciprocate, in this desperate situation, what the other father would have done for him and his children. A further question arises too, then: Would the other father have been sufficiently motivated? If the other would have reneged had their positions been reversed, then the father on the bank loses his rationale from fair reciprocity.

Here, then, the upshot of contractarian thinking deviates from that of utilitarian thinking. Suppose for now that I am right that, if the two could make an agreement with full assurance that the agreement would be kept, they would agree on the arrangement that utilitarianism prescribes. In this way, utilitarianism can stem not only from motives of benevolence, but from motives of fair reciprocity. That's only, though, if the motivations of fair reciprocity are never overwhelmed by other motives, and the parties have full assurance of this.

A contractarianism that heeds the limits of motives of fair reciprocity will be quite different. What would we have agreed on, under the constraint that the motivations we would have to keep the agreement would be sufficiently strong, if everyone knew that the agreement would be kept? That will depend on a psychological question: How strong are motives of fair reciprocity? How strong can we trust them to be under various relevant conditions?

We can see now why there might be a contractarian excuse for rescuing one's own child in preference to two others. If we had been able to make any agreement whatsoever and make it effective, we would have agreed to rescue as many children as possible, no matter whose. But we can't produce such strong motives—and under the constraints of how strong motives of fair reciprocity can be, we wouldn't have made such an agreement only to expect it not to be kept.

I'm touching on what John Rawls called the "strains of commitment."[4] In most of the rest of this lecture, I'll ignore them and explore other questions. I'll consider contractarian arguments that assume full assurance of full compliance, severe though this limitation is. Any full exploration of contractarian arguments, utilitarianism, and moral intuitions, though, would have to pay great heed to the strains of commitment.

The Separateness of Persons

One way of arriving at utilitarianism is to say that morality consists in benevolence, in impartial concern for all involved, including oneself. Rawls responded that impartial benevolence is a weak motive, and that a far stronger motive is fair reciprocity.[5] T. M. Scanlon puts the motive differently: roughly, as a concern to live with others on a basis that no one could reasonably reject.[6] The canoe case suggested a way in which all these might coincide, at least in the case of full compliance. Fair reciprocity consists in abiding by a practice if it's the practice we would have agreed to before we knew who would be in what position. To such a practice, no one could reasonably object.

The question we ask in moral inquiry, I have been saying, isn't the psychological one of what motives we *do* have and how strongly, but the question of what motives *to* have. It's a planning question, a question of how to live with each other. Nothing in the metaethics that I have laid out dictates an answer. Still, the ideals of fair reciprocity and of living with others on a basis they could not reasonably reject seem good candidates for what to want in one's dealings with others. These aims are vague, but I propose to think together with people who might be brought to share these aims, and try to work toward specifying them in a way that might make them worthy of pursuit.

Morality, it is often said, is grounded in respect for persons, and utilitarianism fails in that it can prescribe actions that violate people's rights and fail to respect them. I can't, of course, go over the history of systematic attempts to ground morality in respect and get non-utilitarian conclusions, but my own reading of the history is that these attempts have not had great success—and our brief discussion of the canoe case illustrates why coherent, non-utilitarian theories are so elusive.[7] The vague aims of fair reciprocity and of dealing with others in a way that no one could reasonably reject do strike me as good places to start in working out what aims to have, and what we would have agreed on seems highly relevant to respect and what it demands. I'll be arguing in these lectures that these starting points lead to a moral view that is utilitarian in form, but as I say, considerations of respect are widely

thought to tell against utilitarianism. Before I scrutinize contractarian arguments further, I'll say a few things about why I don't
think respect leads us straightforwardly in directions that oppose
utilitarianism.[8]

Utilitarianism, it is sometimes said, ignores the "separateness of
persons."[9] One person's gain doesn't compensate for another's loss.
A person is not to be sacrificed for the sake of another. Thinking in
terms of "gains" and "losses" or of "sacrifice," though, requires a
base point of comparison, and so we'll need some rationale for
heeding one possible base point as opposed to others. Suppose we
have persons Ida and Jay and states A and B, with Ida better off in
state A and Jay better off in state B. Let's give numbers to how well
off they are:

State	A	B
Ida	9	5
Jay	1	3

Ida's gain in going from state B to state A doesn't compensate for
Jay's loss, so we might try saying: Ida gains, going from 5 to 9 for a
gain of 4, but Jay loses, falling from 3 to 1. Jay has only one life to
lead, and we can't sacrifice him for Ida's benefit. If we frame matters
differently, however, we come to the opposite conclusion: In going
from state A to state B, Ida loses. Jay gains, to be sure, but he and Ida
are separate persons, and Ida can't be sacrificed for Jay.

To chose between these two seeming upshots of the separateness
of persons, we must chose between state A and state B as the base
state from which "gains" and "losses" are measured and "sacrifice"
is attributed. Rawls seemed to choose the state with the worst off
person—state A in this case. That might raise the worry of whether
we can legitimately "sacrifice" the well off to benefit the badly off.
Nozick and some others who appeal to Kant say that we choose as
the base state for comparison the state in which people are entitled
to what they would have.[10] Rawls replies that when the basic
structure of society is at issue, we're asking what entitlements to

institute.[11] Intuitions that invoke ownership and other entitlements are very strong, and they may well be "wired in" to the human psychic makeup.[12] They are very sensitive, though, to "framing" effects: even a person's self-regarding choices are affected by attributing ownership.[13] (Consider "endowment effects": We "give" a person a coffee mug and ask him if he'll trade it for a chocolate bar. He says no. It seems he prefers having the mug to having the chocolate bar. But if we had given him the chocolate bar instead, he would have refused to trade it for the mug. It seems he would then prefer having the chocolate bar to having the mug. The only difference is which of the two objects he frames as already "his."[14]) Can we find some basis for attributing entitlements, then, that is independent of the pragmatic test, independent of evaluating the consequences of a system of entitlements, by a standard that doesn't assume the importance of the entitlements in advance? Nozick tried, but he left the basis of what he was saying unexplained and seemed to appeal to the pragmatic advantages of systems of property.[15]

I conclude that we can't talk of "gains," "losses," and "sacrifice" until we identify some base point for the comparisons. It is true enough that we are separate persons—but nothing about what we may permissibly do follows from that by itself. Our strong intuitions do latch onto some base point or other, but not in any consistent way. Perhaps we could establish some base point as morally relevant. One way to do so, though, would be the way I'll be exploring: ask what we would have agreed to from behind a veil of ignorance, what we would have agreed to treat as morally relevant.

Harsanyi's Theorems

The point of morality, I'm taking it, is to live with each other on a basis that none of us could reasonably reject. No one has a reasonable objection if the system we live by is what we would have agreed to in fair conditions—and one way to make conditions fair is a veil of ignorance. We saw in the canoe case that this may yield utilitarian prescriptions. Harsanyi argued that this upshot generalizes.

His argument starts with the coherence of plans for action as elucidated by classical decision theory. As I discussed in the first lecture, decision theorists have shown that if a way of ranking actions satisfies certain conditions, then it is as if the person chose by maximizing an expected value.[16] It is as if the person formed degrees of credence in the relevant eventualities, attributed levels of value to the various possible outcomes, and then took the alternative that held out the greatest expectation of value, reckoned with those degrees of credence and levels of value. By the "standard conditions" I'll mean any of the various sets of conditions that have been shown to yield the result, and "coherent" plans, I'll assume, are plans that satisfy these conditions. As I indicated in the first lecture, it is highly contentious whether the axioms are requirements of coherence in any ordinary sense of the term, but I'll be exploring what we should think if they are.

Harsanyi proved two theorems that I'll call his two welfare theorems. His first welfare theorem concerned something like Rawls's "original position" with his "veil of ignorance."[17] Think of valid moral rules as the rules one would choose assuming an equal chance of being anyone. Assume one's preferences are coherent, in that they satisfy the standard conditions. Then one will prefer the rules that would yield the greatest total utility. Here by "individual utility," I mean the scale that represents one's preferences given that one will turn out to be that person.[18]

Harsanyi's second welfare theorem is this: Suppose that prospective individual benefit is coherent, and so is desirability from a moral point of view. Suppose also that morality is for humanity in at least the following sense: If one prospect is better than a second for each individual, it is the better prospect ethically. (This is a version of what is called the *prospective Pareto condition*.) Then desirability from a moral point of view, he proved, is a weighted sum of individual benefits.[19] The only way ethical evaluation could satisfy these conditions and depart from utilitarianism is by weighing one person's benefit more than another.

Economists represent the theorem in graphical form. We take the simple case of two people. Each social order we might have instituted gives each person a prospective benefit, and we can represent this benefit by a point, with Ida's benefit the x-coordinate and Jay's the y-coordinate. These, we can say, are the combinations of prospects that were feasible. The feasible combinations that satisfy the prospective Pareto condition, such that no alternative would have given both people better prospects at once, lie along the frontier at the upper right. A moral theory that is consistent with the prospective Pareto condition chooses one of the points on this frontier as that of the just social order. This point, though, maximizes some weighted combination of the individuals' prospective benefits. Graphically, we can see that it is maximally extreme in some direction (see figure 1). Harsanyi's second welfare theorem is that a combination that satisfied his three conditions has this property.

The challenge to anyone who wants to get a non-utilitarian morality out of thought on a social contract is how to evade the force of Harsanyi's two theorems. If you are going to be a non-utilitarian, you will adopt moral rules that none of us would have chosen for his own sake unless he knew of some special way that he and not others stood to benefit. And any evaluation of the prospects that various different moral orders bring must either (i) violate some demand of rationality, or (ii) weigh one person's utility above another's, or (iii) rank some prospect best even though another one prospectively benefits everyone more.

Now Harsanyi's two welfare theorems have been much discussed, if not sufficiently. The quick, careless statements of the theorems that I have given would require close scrutiny, and important parts of the needed scrutiny are in print.[20] What I can hope to do

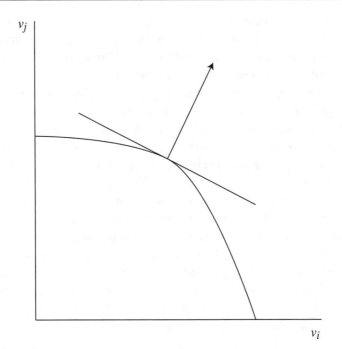

Figure 1

is just to select a few issues that are relevant to these debates, framing the theorems as parts of moral inquiry as I have been picturing it.

A Person's Good

What is a person's good or benefit? In the tradition that Harsanyi worked in, a person's good is a matter of her preferences. We gauge the strength of her preferences by the preferences she would have among risky prospects: If you would risk a one-in-a-million chance of being killed by a car, but no more, to cross the street and buy a chocolate bar, then the benefit to you of a chocolate bar counts as one-millionth the harm to you of being killed. This notion of benefit has three chief problems. One seems tractable enough: Philosophers hasten to add that the preferences must be considered and informed. A second problem is more difficult: The preferences of any decent person won't just be for that person's own benefit. The person will care about others; he will care about fairness; he will care, perhaps, about living with others on a basis that no one could reasonably reject. A person's benefit is at best one component of his considered, informed preferences. What component is that?

The third problem interacts with the second. What people prefer for themselves differs from person to person. Some differences aren't fundamental: I dislike asparagus and my wife loves it, and so I prefer not to eat it and my wife prefers to eat it. Basically, though, we both want to enjoy our food, and we're different in what we enjoy. For the case of being her with her tastes, I want to eat asparagus. Other examples, though, might be different. When I lived in Ghana, people told me that one thing they set great store on was a big funeral. That puzzled me, but as I thought about it, I realized that a big funeral indicates how one is loved and respected in the community, and to be loved, respected, and missed did seem to me to be things a person could intelligibly put great stock in. Still, once we distinguish carefully what goes on in one's life and what happens after, people may differ in whether they care, for their own sake, how they are regarded after death.

When I stand behind a veil of ignorance and choose a social ethos to institute, I contemplate that I may turn out to be you with your basic preferences, and I may turn out to be me with my basic preferences. You and I may differ even in the basic preferences we would have if our preferences were fully considered and informed. Rawls stressed this and proposed that instead of looking to self-regarding preferences, we look to what he called an "index of primary social goods." Primary goods he defined as things a rational person wants whatever else he wants.[21] Saying all this, however, leaves it as part of his project to find some basis for this index. Rawls thought that the problem was mitigated by his theory, since he only had to deal in broad categories like income and opportunities, and only had to identify whether the worst off were better off under one arrangement than under another. In fact, though, his theory ends up placing great demands on this index. What turns out to matter, in his theory, is the life prospects of those in the worst starting positions in life. To tote up uncertain prospects, we need more than an ordering from best outcomes to worst. We need to know what differences are big and what are small. We need what measurement theorists call a cardinal scale, and we need to be able to compare people on this scale. I am asking about the basis we might have for making these comparisons.[22]

As for Scanlon, he rejects the kind of prospective argument that lies at the center of Rawls's "Original Position" and Harsanyi's theorems.[23] I myself have followed Harsanyi and Rawls in their proposals for how we can dismiss some objections as unreasonable. You do something and I object. You reply, "That's the established way we do things, and that's what you would have wanted before you knew which of us you would be and so how in particular it would affect you." This seems to show my objection unreasonable, and from crediting such dismissals, Harsanyi draws powerful consequences. We are now seeing, though, that he must place great demands on the notion of individual benefit.

In his book *What We Owe to Each Other*, Scanlon offers an extended critique of the notion of "welfare," or a person's "good." I view this critique as raising the most serious problem for the line of argument I am examining, and so it is this critique that I will discuss.[24] This particular critique, even if successful, doesn't entirely rule out the possibility of dismissing objections as unreasonable on prospective grounds in the kind of way I have been discussing.[25] It does, though, place on an advocate of such tests the burden of saying what notion of benefit can play this role. Scanlon allows that conceptions of how well off a person is might be tailored to play a role in a moral theory.[26] Clearly, though, from the way he himself develops his test, he doesn't think the test of what we would have wanted from behind a veil of ignorance plays anything like the broad and systematic role in a coherent moral theory that Harsanyi thought it played. Scanlon's critique of the concept of a person's good is a serious one, and I'll be particularly concerned to grapple with it.

I'll be arguing that we can't derive the needed notion of individual benefit directly from the preferences that people have, or even the preferences they would have in ideal conditions. Instead, forming a conception of benefit is part of ethical thinking, part of thinking how to live among other people. That fits a part of what Scanlon himself concludes,[27] but if the retort I've imagined always deflates a claim that an objection is reasonable, then thought of prospective benefit may have a much larger role in coherent ethical thinking than Scanlon gives it.

Preferences for Being Another

To illustrate and explore the problem, let's return to the simple, toy case of Ida and Jay. I'll suppose first that we understand the notion of a person's good. Suppose again that how well off Ida and Jay would be in states A and B goes as follows:

Structure	A	B
Ida	9	5
Jay	1	3
Expected	5	4

Harsanyi's argument favors structure A. Before they both knew who they would be, both would prefer structure A with expected level 5 to structure B with expected level 4. Jay comes out badly under structure A, but if A is the going structure, he has no reasonable objection to it.

I now turn to the objection raised by Gauthier, Suzumura, and others.[28] What do the numbers in my simple table represent? They represent evaluations from behind a veil of ignorance, made by people, as we imagine it, who are choosing a basic social structure only for their own prospective benefit. We are asking what notion of benefit feeds into the moral force of the rejoinder, "That's the structure you would have chosen for your own benefit." Ida, from behind the veil of ignorance, contemplates two possibilities: that she will be Ida and that she will be Jay. Now Ida in the world, let's suppose, wants a big funeral, and in state A she gets it, whereas in state B she doesn't. Does she have this preference behind the veil of ignorance? Suppose she does, but that Jay doesn't. Jay understands well enough that, in case he turns out to be Ida, his actual strongest concerns include having a big funeral. But being Jay, he doesn't intrinsically care about having a big funeral. He is indifferent between being Ida and having a big funeral and being Ida and unexpectedly being cremated after death without ceremony. Being Ida, he understands, includes wanting a big funeral, but as he is, behind the veil, he is indifferent between (a) wanting a big funeral and getting it and (b) wanting a big funeral and not getting it. "If I get it," he figures, "I won't be around to enjoy it, and if I don't get it, I'll never miss it."

Once we distinguish Ida's preference for being Ida in A from Jay's preference for being Ida in A, we might get a more complex table like the one shown in table 1. Ida's evaluation of being Ida under structure A includes 4 units for having a big funeral and 5 for other aspects of how things go for her. Jay's evaluation of being Ida under structure A includes only the 5 units from those other aspects. From behind the veil, he places no value on actually having a big funeral in case he is Ida.

Ida now can't refute Jay's objection by saying that A is the state he would have chosen if he hadn't known who he would be. The state he would have chosen is B, which gives him an expected utility of 4 as opposed to 3. Suppose, though, that structure B has been

Table 1

Ida's preferences for being			Jay's preferences for being		
in state	*A*	*B*	in state	*A*	*B*
being Ida	9	5	being Ida	5	5
being Jay	1	3	being Jay	1	3
expectation	5	4	*expectation*	3	4

instituted, and Ida, not getting a big funeral, objects. (Or since she's not around to object, suppose someone objects on her behalf.) Jay can't deflate the objection by saying that *B* is the structure she would have chosen if she hadn't known who she would turn out to be. For each state there is an objection that can't be shown unreasonable, at least in this way. Unless we can find some other way to show one of the objections unreasonable, we're damned whichever state we institute.

That fits in with Scanlon's critique. There is no one coherent notion, he says, that will do the jobs that "welfare" or "a person's good" has been asked to do in much ethical thinking: roughly, determining (i) what a person will choose insofar as others aren't affected, (ii) what others concerned to benefit him will choose to promote, and (iii) what counts as the person's good for purposes of moral thinking.[29] We are asking about (iii), and indeed, as Scanlon told us, not finding a way to read off a person's good from her preferences.

An appealing way out might be to let Ida be the judge of her own good. The problem remains, though—as Rawls insisted. From behind the veil of ignorance, in his system, we are choosing among alternative basic structures of society. What people will want, at base, might be highly affected by the kind of society we choose to have been nurtured in. Ida might have been indifferent to a big funeral if she had grown up in a different sort of society, in an alternative social order from among those that are open to choice from behind the veil of ignorance.

Rawls, as I say, was responding partly to this kind of problem when he set up his "index of primary social goods," but he offered, I think, no adequate, defensible rationale for this solution. I am asking whether such a rationale can be provided.

The Question of a Person's Good

Let's call the retort I've been discussing the "You'd have agreed" retort. This retort to an objection, recall, has two elements. First, "That's the way we do things." What you object to is a feature of our going practice. Second, "Before you knew how you in particular would turn out to be affected, you would have agreed to the practice—and for your own advantage." This retort does seem to have moral force.[30] Some notion of advantage and disadvantage, moreover, seems hard to escape in our moral thinking. Objections to a social order often are on the grounds that it disadvantages someone unfairly. Such an objection itself appeals to a notion of advantage or benefit, and so if the retort is incoherent because it requires a notion of a person's good, then so was the original objection. Still, we are left to ask what kind of force to accord a retort like this. The retort so far is vague; how can we spell it out in any precise way that will carry moral force?

Our question concerns the basic moral arrangements by which we live together. If we are to make sense of what we would have agreed to, we can't just look to our aims as they are as a result of the basic moral arrangements we have. The retort, if it is to have specific content, must be filled in with coherent fundamental aims we can take ourselves to have from a standpoint that doesn't just take us as we are. We must be able look to the various sorts of people we might have turned out to be under various different social circumstances and ask how well these fundamental aims for oneself are fulfilled in these various kinds of lives. Will a plan for living with others, then, respect the "You'd have agreed" retort under some such interpretation?

In the rest of this lecture, I'll be considering one particular kind of way to work out the contractarian ideal, the ideal of living with others, if one can, on a basis that no one could reasonably reject. The way is to take the "You'd have agreed" retort and give it an interpretation suitable for answering fundamental moral questions. I won't settle what the interpretation should be. (I wish I could, but I can't.) Nor will I establish that this is the only fully coherent way to work out the idea of a basis for living together that no one could reasonably reject. What I'll be doing, rather, is to characterize a plan for living that incorporates such an interpretation of the ideal.

I plan to live with others, if I can, in mutual respect, on a basis that no one could reasonably reject on his own behalf. This plan constitutes an intuition on how to live with others, and as a plan, it can be couched as an imperative.

> Prefer most to live with others on a basis that no one could reasonably reject on his own behalf.

The intuition, though, is vague; crucial terms in the plan are left unexplained. We must specify what it is to reject a basis for living with each other *reasonably* and *on one's own behalf*. Harsanyi and Rawls offer an interpretation, a partial standard for what disqualifies an objection as unreasonable. In thinking how to live with each other, we may fill in our plan for living with each other with their proposal. Here is a partial interpretation of the indeterminate plan, a way to fill in the plan to live with others on a basis that no one could reasonably reject on his own behalf.

> A rejection on one's own behalf of a going social arrangement is unreasonable if, absent information about which person one would turn out to be, one would have rationally chosen that arrangement on one's own behalf.

This specification of one's plan for living with others, though, is still badly incomplete. It leaves to be explained choosing a thing "on one's own behalf" or for one's own sake. Uninformatively, we can put this in terms of a person's good.

> One chooses rationally on one's own behalf only if one chooses what is prospectively most to one's good.

The Total Good of People

A plan that satisfies the three conditions I have stated will be a plan to maximize the total good of people. For suppose that one's plan satisfies these conditions, and consider a social arrangement that for each person, absent information about who he is, is most to his prospective good. Everyone would choose this arrangement on his own behalf, and so no one could reasonably object to it on his own behalf. A plan that satisfies these three conditions, then, will require living with others on this basis. Now for a fixed population, as Harsanyi's first welfare theorem showed, the basis for living with others that is most to one's prospective good behind a veil of ignorance is the basis that maximizes prospects for the total good of people. The plan that satisfies these three conditions, then, is a plan to maximize prospects for the sum total good of people.

The three conditions left us, though, with an uninterpreted term, the term 'good' in the phrase 'my good' or 'your good.' Scanlon's challenge is to find an interpretation of this notion of a person's good that lets it play a role in these axioms. What constitute preferences on one's own behalf? The requirement on such an interpretation is a planning requirement: We need an interpretation that goes some way to fill out how to live with each other on a basis of mutual respect. A person will be convinced of the interpretation if she plans to want most to live with others on a basis of mutual respect as so interpreted. I hope, then, to address people who, like me, plan vaguely to live with others on a basis of mutual respect if we can, and I follow Harsanyi and Rawls in proposing a form that such a plan might take. The question for each of us is then whether to live in a way that takes this form.

This gives us a meaning for talk of a person's "good." A person's *good*, we can try saying, is whatever plays this role in the way to live. We accept that there is such a thing as a person's good when we restrict our plans for how to live with each other to ones that take the form displayed in the axioms. We accept some particular answer to the question "What is a person's good?" when we plan to live with others in a way that fits the axioms. What we regard as a person's "good" is then whatever plays the role of a person's "good" in the plan we have that fits those axioms. The interpretation we then accept is whatever interpretation of the axioms we plan to live by.

Notice, I have been speaking, so far, not of what really does constitute a person's good, but of what it is to *accept* an answer to the question of what constitutes a person's good. The question of what constitutes a person's good is, I have been saying, a planning question. The meaning of a planning term can't be given a straight, naturalistic definition, in terms suited to empirical psychology. All we can say in straight terms is this: "A person's good is whatever it is, if anything, that figures in the way to live with others in a certain way. That way is specified by the three axioms. Whatever plays that role in the way to live, if anything does, is a person's good." What we can say further about the concept can only be oblique. We can say what it is for a person to *think* or *regard* something as constituting a person's good. To do so is to have a plan for living that takes the form of the axioms. What one then regards as a person's good is whatever plays the role given by the term 'good' in those axioms.

The string of three conditions is a formal constraint on how to live with others. The constraint is to live with others on some specification or other of the ideal of fair reciprocity. Which specification is a further planning question, a further question of how to live with others.

If our preferences for how to live, as we struggle to make them coherent, do take this form, then we can go on to argue, using Harsanyi's first welfare theorem, that behind the veil of ignorance, one would choose the social arrangement that, in prospect, maximizes the sum of people's goods. Preferring to live on that basis, one prefers to do one's part in an order that maximizes the total good of people, provided that everyone else can be fully expected to do so.

Is There Such a Thing as a Person's Good?

In this lecture I have been drawing on Harsanyi's first welfare theorem and applying it to interpret the appeal of Scanlon's talk of what no one could reasonably reject. The interpretation I proposed is one that Scanlon himself would repudiate, and nothing I have drawn from Harsanyi in this lecture shows Scanlon to be incoherent in this. It remains to be seen whether there is a coherent alternative to the kind of interpretation I have been proposing.

I hope, though, that I have given some glimmering of what speaks for Scanlon's reasonable rejection test when it is given an interpretation that takes this form. I interpreted the test as assessing rejections on one's own behalf. A rejection with moral force, my assumption was, must be a rejection on behalf of someone or other—and if it is on behalf of someone other than the person who does the rejecting, the question becomes whether that other person could reject the arrangement reasonably. The ideal, then, is to live with others, if one can, under an arrangement that everyone adheres to voluntarily, because it is an arrangement that no one could reasonably reject on his own behalf.

Talk of doing things on one's own behalf amounts to talk of doing them for one's own good as one sees it. Scanlon challenges traditional ways that ethical theorists have used the notion of a person's good and so challenges the intelligibility of such talk. On the account I have given, the question of whether there is such a thing as a person's good is a planning question. It is a question of whether to live in a way that takes a certain form. I come to a view about what a person's good is, then, if and when I come to have preferences that take this form. We come to a joint view, in discussion, of what a person's good is if we all come to have preferences that take this form, and—crucially—for each of us the same valuations play the role these conditions assign to a person's good.

So far, this may well fit in with what Scanlon would expect. One of the functions that the notion of well-being has been meant to serve, he says, is "to be the basis on which an individual's interests are taken into account in moral argument."[31] Moral principles will do such jobs, though, he thinks, with a variety of notions of a person's interests or good, and no single one of these notions will play the comprehensive moral role of being what the correct moral theory tells us in general to distribute.[32] I am now saying that *if* there is something that plays this comprehensive role, then that is what counts as a person's good. We are still left, though, with the question of whether anything does. My own proposed interpretation of Scanlon's reasonable rejection test supposed that there is, but it is an interpretation he himself rejects, and I have not shown that it was the only possible coherent interpretation.

In the next lecture, I turn from Harsanyi's first welfare theorem to his second. I ask how it constrains the ideal social contract—the arrangement for living together, if any, that no one could reasonably reject. This theorem, I'll argue, can be interpreted in a way that makes it compelling, and in that form, the theorem and a variant of it do sharply constrain what the ideal social contract could be.

Notes

1. Frankena, *Ethics* (1963), p. 98.
2. Sidgwick, *Methods of Ethics* (1907).
3. Jeske and Fumerton (1997), "Relatives and Relativism."

4. Rawls, *Theory of Justice* (1971), pp. 145, 177–78, 490–504. My discussions of Rawls in these lectures refer to this version of his theory, although I think they apply to later versions as well.

5. Rawls, ibid., pp. 494–95, 500.

6. Scanlon: *What We Owe to Each Other* (1998). More precisely, contractualism, he tell us, "holds that an act is wrong if its performance under the circumstances would be disallowed by any set of principles for the general regulation of behavior that no one could reasonably reject as a basis for informed, unforced general agreement" (153).

7. Kant, *Grundlegung* (1785). Smith, "Rawls and Utilitarianism" (1980), is a fine discussion of whether Rawls succeeds in finding a rationale for a non-utilitarian theory. In my "Morality As Consistency" (1999), I look at Korsgaard's attempt to derive a Kantian morality; see her *Sources of Normativity* (1996).

8. Frankena, in "Ethics of Respect" (1986), argues that the content of morality must be settled in order to determine what constitutes treating a person with respect, so that the demands of respect can't be the basis of morality.

9. See Rawls, *Theory of Justice* (1971), pp. 26–31. "The most natural way" to arrive at utilitarianism, he says, is "to adopt for society as a whole the principle of rational choice for one man." This is not the only way, he says, but he concludes, "Utilitarianism does not take seriously the distinction between persons" (pp. 26–27).

10. Nozick, *Anarchy, State, and Utopia* (1974). He discusses whether the rich don't have the same right to complain of Rawls's difference principle as the poor would have to complain of making the best off as well off as possible, pp. 190–97. Elsewhere he speaks of "sacrifice" (pp. 32–33).

11. Rawls, "Basic Structure As Subject" (1977). See his *Theory of Justice* (1971), pp. 7–10.

12. Fiske, in "Four Elementary Forms" (1992), argues that people use four "elementary relational models" to coordinate social interaction; he calls them Communal Sharing, Authority Ranking, Equality Matching, and Market Pricing. The universality suggests genetic adaptation to think of social relations in terms of these

schemas. Concepts of property are obviously involved in Market Pricing, and they are also involved in aspects of some of the others. Gifts come under Communal Sharing, and Equality Matching includes matching of contributions.

13. On "framing" effects, see Tversky and Kahneman, "The Framing of Decisions" (1981).

14. Kahneman, Knetch, and Thaler (1990).

15. Nozick, *Anarchy, State, and Utopia* (1974). For critiques along this line, see Varian, "Distributive Justice" (1975), and my "Natural Property Rights" (1977). See also Sidgwick, *Methods of Ethics* (1907), pp. 278–83.

16. Ramsey, "Truth and Probability" (1931); Savage, *Foundations of Statistics* (1954).

17. Rawls used these terms in *Theory of Justice* (1971).

18. Harsanyi, "Cardinal Utility" (1953). The term 'utility' is often defined differently from the way I define it here; one frequent meaning would let the person's "utility" be the scale that represents the preferences of that person himself. I consider later in this lecture why the two senses might diverge.

19. Harsanyi, "Cardinal Welfare" (1955), p. 313. See Broome, *Weighing Goods* (1991), for a superb treatment of this theorem and its ethical implications. Harsanyi spoke of individual "preferences" and implicitly assumed that they characterize individual good or benefit; I discuss this shortly. Broome distinguishes questions of good and questions of preference. He confines the term 'Pareto condition' to one couched in terms of preferences and calls the principle as I have stated it the "Principle of Personal Good" (p. 155). Harsanyi's two theorems, understood as abstract mathematical results, can of course be given more than one interpretation in their applications to ethical questions, and each interpretation would require separate scrutiny. Broome calls Harsanyi's second welfare theorem, under the interpretation I am giving it, the "Interpersonal Addition Theorem" (pp. 162–63).

20. For critiques of Harsanyi, see especially Broome, *Weighing Goods* (1991). See also Gauthier, in "Refutation of Utilitarianism" (1982), and Suzumura, "Interpersonal Comparisons" (1997).

21. Rawls, *Theory of Justice* (1971), esp. pp. 62, 92.

22. Rawls, *Theory of Justice* (1971), pp. 64, 76–83, 93–98. I discuss problems of characterizing a representative person with the resources that Rawls allows himself in "Disparate Goods" (1979).

23. Scanlon, "Contractualism and Utilitarianism" (1982). I thank Frances Kamm for reminding me of Scanlon's critique of Harsanyi in this paper. She and I discuss the points Scanlon makes in her commentary and my reply.

24. Scanlon, "Status of Well-Being" (1998); *What We Owe* (1998), chap. 3. One excuse I have for scrutinizing the ethical import of Harsanyi's two welfare theorems, when Broome, in *Weighing Goods* (1991), has given such a thorough treatment of the issues, is that Scanlon's critique calls into question the notion of a person's good that is central to Broome's argument and that Broome mostly takes as granted.

25. Scanlon, as I say, does have other arguments that he thinks do rule out this test, but those are not the arguments I am referring to here.

26. Scanlon, *What We Owe* (1998), p. 110. He gives Rawls's primary social goods and Sen's capability sets as examples of such conceptions.

27. Scanlon, *What We Owe* (1998), p. 110. It also fits Broome, *Weighing Goods* (1991), p. 220.

28. Gauthier, in "Refutation of Utilitarianism" (1982); Broome, *Weighing Goods* (1991), p. 55; Suzumura, "Interpersonal Comparisons" (1997). I discuss some of these issues in "Interpersonal Comparisons" (1986).

29. Scanlon, *What We Owe* (1998), chap. 3 (pp. 108–43).

30. Barry, *Theories of Justice* (1989), pp. 334–35, questions the moral significance of Harsanyi's first welfare theorem, as does Broome quoting Barry in *Weighing Goods* (1991), pp. 56–57. To my own moral sensibility, the theorem has the moral significance that I am indicating.

31. Scanlon, *What We Owe* (1998), p. 136.

32. Scanlon, *What We Owe* (1998), pp. 138–40.

III. Common Goals and the Ideal Social Contract

In the first lecture, I proposed an account of what our job is in ethical theory. It is one of planning how to live with each other. Each of us plans how to live with others, and how to feel about things that he and others do or might do. With regard to planning, I cited a family of arguments from twentieth-century decision theory, the arguments of Ramsey, Savage, Hammond, and others. These arguments start with requirements of coherence in planning. They conclude that any ideally coherent planner in effect maximizes expected value on some scale. We could represent her plans, that is to say, by ascribing (i) numerical probabilities to eventualities and (ii) numerical values to possible outcomes, and then evaluate each strategy for living by the values of the outcomes that it might have, each weighted by its probability. It has been controversial whether the conditions on plans that these arguments invoke are genuinely requirements of coherence, but I haven't seriously entered into those debates. Rather, I have been concerned with what follows if this tradition in decision theory is right.

In the second lecture, I cited two other major twentieth-century findings, Harsanyi's two welfare theorems. The theorems seem to show that the only coherent ethical theory is utilitarian in form. Utilitarians judge social arrangements by the total benefit they deliver. Specifically, Harsanyi's second welfare theorem placed three conditions on evaluating prospects: that (i) evaluations of prospective individual benefit are coherent, (ii) ethical evaluations of prospects are coherent, and (iii) anything that is prospectively better for everyone is prospectively better ethically. Harsanyi showed, from these conditions, that if ethics treats everyone alike, then ethical value is a sum of individual benefits.

Equipped with this theorem, I took up the planning question of how to live with others—restricting myself to plans that place a premium on living with each other on a basis of mutual respect. I took up Scanlon's proposed interpretation of this standard: to live with each other on a basis that no one could reasonably reject. I explored how far the "You'd have agreed" retort could be taken, and this led to the aim that Harsanyi and Rawls propose. The aim is to live with others on a basis that we would have agreed to in ideally fair conditions, each with a view to his own prospective good—provided that this way of living together is the established way we do things. All this gives us at most a fragment of a plan for living with others, a plan for the case of "full compliance." It applies, that is to say, to the special case where our established ways of living together are the ones we would have chosen in fair conditions.

This interpretation of contractarianism, though, helps itself to talk of an individual's good. We must ask whether there is any conception of a person's good that makes the contractarian ideal, so interpreted, an ideal to plan for. If there is, then Harsanyi's first welfare theorem seems conclusive. If one's preferences in ideally fair conditions are coherent and one doesn't expect more to be one person than another, then one in effect values each outcome as the sum of the way one values it in case one is each of the people that, for all one knows, one is. At this point, however, enters Scanlon's critique: Though loose talk of a person's good makes rough and ready sense, there's no one thing, he argues, that plays all the roles that have traditionally been ascribed to a person's good (or to welfare, utility, interest, benefit, or the like). I in effect accepted much of this critique. One role that Scanlon does allow to the notion of a person's good or interests, however, is that of counting in a particular way for particular moral purposes. (An example is Rawls's index of "primary social goods" such as money, powers, and opportunities.) As Scanlon himself works out his "contractualism," no highly general notion of a person's good or interests plays any comprehensive role. I am asking whether Scanlon is right about this. In particular, do Harsanyi's welfare theorems compel us to develop a conception of a person's good or interests and then conclude that morality consists in promoting a general interest—a value composed of individual interests? Is it incoherent to think otherwise, once we think that morality is made for humanity?

The main point of the second lecture was still to ask *about* the questions we are asking. I looked at two questions: First, is there any such coherent thing as a person's good? Second, if so, what is it? What is a person's good? These both, I said, are planning questions. We interpret talk of "person *i*'s good" when we say what form a person's preferences must take for him to think that there is such a thing, and have an opinion as to what a person's good is. I thus characterized, in indirect terms, what a person's good is if there is any such thing.

If we start out taking the concept of a person's good or benefit as intelligible, then Harsanyi's second welfare theorem, even more than the first, makes it hard to see how Scanlon's reasonable rejection test could lead to anything but agreeing to maximize the total prospective good of persons. We would reasonably reject a social arrangement if it is wasteful, if some alternative would give us each a greater prospective benefit. Our conception of individual social benefit is presumably coherent. As for prospective ethical value, I'll discuss that briefly later, but suppose for now that we would agree to a coherent conception of value from the ethical point of view. That gives us all the conditions of Harsanyi's second welfare theorem. If we treat everyone's good alike, the theorem then says, we agree to maximize the total good of everyone.

What now, though, if the very notion of a person's good is in question? Still, I'll argue in this lecture, Harsanyi's second welfare theorem (or something close to it) tells us the form that a coherent social contract will take—its formal structure. Doing this leaves open the question of how to fill the structure in. Harsanyi's second welfare theorem, like the first, is in part an abstract mathematical result, which can be given various interpretations. Harsanyi had his own interpretation, but even if the assumptions of the theorem don't all hold under that interpretation, they might all hold under another. Both theorems are mathematically correct, and so the debate must be over whether any interpretation of these mathematical results is of ethical import. Specifically, is there any interpretation under which Harsanyi's second welfare theorem shows that a coherent ethics must take something like a utilitarian form?

Much of ethical theory, over the last few decades, has been devoted to showing that there are things to care about and to want others to care about, in living with each other, that don't take the form of summing up the good of individuals, under any conception of what a person's good consists in. Each person has special concerns and responsibilities and shouldn't be expected just to place them on a par with the concerns and responsibilities of everyone else. The Jeske and Fumerton canoe example was meant to give vivid intuitive support to such a picture of the demands of morality. Harsanyi's second welfare theorem, though, I'll be arguing, shows that this anti-utilitarian picture won't fit in with contractarian thinking.

I am taking it, remember, that Hammond's argument, or another like it, establishes that requirements of decision-theoretic coherence apply to the totality of aims that a person has reason to advance, the totality of considerations for a person to weigh in making his decisions. It doesn't immediately follow that there is such a thing as the self-interested component of those aims, and Scanlon may be denying that it follows at all. I will argue that it does follow—but my argument will be indirect.

The Kingdom of Ends

By the *ideal social contract*, I mean the way of living together that no one could reasonably reject. (I'll ignore the question of whether there is such a way or whether there might be more than one such way.) Suppose, then, for the sake of inquiry, that Scanlon is right, and the ideal social contract doesn't take the form of settling what is to count as a person's good, and then agreeing each to advance the sum of everyone's good. What possibilities does that leave open?

Here is a first question about the ideal social contract: The contract places constraints on the ways each of us is to pursue his aims. These constraints must be ones that it is rational for each of us to abide by, given that this particular social contract spells out our established ways of living with each other, and given the rationality of wanting to live together on a basis of mutual respect—interpreted as living in ways that no one could reasonably reject. Suppose, then, each of us acts rationally and abides by those constraints. Since we abide by the constraints rationally and voluntarily, our plan of action, in light of this contract's being in force, is coherent. That entails, we are supposing, that it satisfies the Hammond conditions and amounts to maximizing expected value on some scale. Here, then, is the question: Are we all, under the ideal social contract, to have a common set of aims? Does the agreement we would have arrived at, in ideally fair conditions, take the form of agreeing to a common set of aims—aims that somehow accommodate what each of us has reason to want in life? Would our agreement be each to maximize expected value on the same scale? (If so, then what's up for negotiation in arriving at the social contract is what this common scale is to be.) Or alternatively, would our agreement allow each of us to pursue her own set of aims, different from the aims of others but somehow constrained to accommodate things that others have reason to want?

We are asking about what Kant dubbed the "kingdom of ends." On the predominant interpretation of Kant, the kingdom of ends is an arrangement that each of us wills, whereby we can each pursue our separate ends in a way that duly accommodates the ends of others. This reading fits much of what Kant says. An alternative, though, would be to conceive the kingdom of ends in a more utilitarian way, with each of us accommodating the ends of others by incorporating them into her own aims, weighing the ends of each person equally in her decisions. She still pursues her own ends, in that her ends count in equally with everyone else's. Others too count her ends equally with theirs—but normally, of course, she is in the best position to advance her own ends. Clearly Kant rejected this as what he meant by the kingdom of ends, but the question remains whether any other systematic sense can be given to the ideal.[1]

Now as an interpretation of the ideal social contract, the first alternative, I'll argue—allowing us each to pursue a different set of aims—is incoherent. Suppose the ideal social contract did take this form. Each of us, we have agreed, is free to have various aims that satisfy the conditions of our agreement, different from the aims that are to guide the decisions of others. We each adopt such a separate set of goals, suppose. Since we act rationally in doing so, the goals can be represented as a scale of value to be pursued. Call this the person's *goal-scale*. My goal-scale, note, doesn't then represent just my own good in any normal sense of the term. It makes some accommodation of my ends to the ends of others—to their good, or to other things they have reason to want. The scale presumably puts great weight, for instance, on not killing you, even if I could get away with it and even if killing you would greatly advance things I have reason to want. My goal-scale thus accommodates your end of not being murdered, whether that end is to my own good or not.[2]

My interests, in some sense, will figure into my goal-scale, but they won't be all that determines it—and my interests figure somehow into the goal-scales of others too. That is the sort of thing that, on this conception, an ideal social contract would require.

Now the problem for such a social contract is that diverging goal-scales can make for prisoner's dilemmas. That is to say, there will be cases where one prospect X comes out higher on everyone's goal-scale than does another prospect Y, but where if each of us guides his choices by his own goal-scale, we will end up with prospect Y. We could, in such a case, have agreed on a shared goal-scale that would end us up with X. Thus whatever is to be said from my point of view for coming higher on my goal-scale, and whatever is to be said from your point of view for coming higher on your goal-scale, there's more to be said from both our points of view for X than for Y—and yet the social contract tells us to act in ways that combine to achieve Y. This seems an incoherent way to arrange our lives, a way with no intelligible rationale. Any of us can reasonably reject the arrangement as wasteful of that which is worth his pursuing.

The work here is being done by Harsanyi's second welfare theorem under a new interpretation—or more precisely, by a variant of the theorem. Consider first the original theorem on this new reading: An individual's prospects we now read as his goal-scale, the scale on which he acts, in light of the social contract, to maximize prospects. Harsanyi's first condition thus becomes simply that each individual has a coherent policy for action, representable by a goal-scale. The second condition of the theorem, the prospective Pareto condition, we now read as ruling out a social arrangement if some alternative comes higher on everyone's goal-scale. The third condition is now that social policy be coherent.

This third condition, though, is open to question, and handling this issue requires not precisely Harsanyi's theorem but a variant. For our purposes, it turns out, we can drop the third condition. Consider all the prospects we could jointly bring into being by each adopting a complete contingency plan for action. Consider any one of those prospects that satisfies the prospective Pareto condition. There will be a goal-scale that is a weighted average of individuals' goal-scales for which this prospect comes highest.[3] Thus, we can argue, if individuals abiding by the social contract have distinct goal-scales, and if collectively their policies for action yield a prospect that satisfies the prospective Pareto condition in terms of their respective goal-scales, then there is a possible common goal-scale that they could have reached this outcome by adopting.

I'm not now appealing to any suspect notion of a person's good. Even if there is such a thing as a person's good, his goal-scale, as I have said, represents not just his own good. Rather, it reflects all that he has reason to aim for, given that the established ways of doing things accord with an ideal contract, and given that he has reason to abide by this established social contract voluntarily. I am not now assuming that, in agreeing on the social contract, each of us would be concerned solely to advance his own good. I'm appealing, rather, to an incoherence in the rationale for any social contract that allows us to pursue goals that might conflict.

I began, in the first two lectures, with schematic cases of children needing rescue. These weren't cases, note, where it is clear what constitutes a father's good. The grounds we recognize for a father to have special concern for his own children aren't just a matter of the gratification he gets from them and the anguish of losing them, but of special parental responsibilities. Indeed if we ask what component of a parent's concern for a child is self-interested, the question may have no clear sense. Still, as we saw, whatever special reasons a father has to want his own children in particular not to drown—reasons he doesn't share with fathers of other children—those aims may be better advanced in prospect by a social contract that tells us each to weigh the safety of others' children as he does the safety of his own. I am now saying that this lesson generalizes. Any social arrangement that lets us pursue divergent goals suffers a like incoherence. Whatever reasons each has for the peculiarities of her own goals, there is a way better to advance, in prospect, all those goals at once. The way is to agree on a common scale of goals for all to pursue. The way is to agree, as we might put it, on what to treat as the overall good, and then for each of us to advance the overall good as much as possible.

By *the overall good*, then, I shall mean good as measured by whatever goal-scale would be specified by the ideal social contract. It is whatever goal-scale it would be unreasonable for anyone to reject as the one we are each to take as his own. The scale that gauges the overall good is the one we would agree to use, in effect, to guide our decisions. We would agree always to do whatever offers the best prospects as measured by that scale. We would agree, that is to say, to do whatever maximizes the rationally expected value of the overall good.

The Common Ends to Adopt

A social contract with a coherent rationale, I have been arguing, will designate a goal-scale for us to adopt in common. What I'm to advance, you too are to advance. But what will this common goal-scale consist in? It must somehow take all of us into account. Morality, after all, is made for humanity, not the other way around. If a person is reasonably to reject a proposed arrangement, it must be on the basis of something a person has reason to want from a social contract. If this isn't the person's own good, or if there isn't any such definite thing as a person's own good, the basis must still be something worth wanting—worth wanting from that person's own standpoint and on grounds that don't invoke preconceived demands of morality.

To say all this, though, is not to specify just how the overall good takes us into account. What is this overall good to consist in? This question, if what I have been saying is right, is a planning question, a question of what to want from a social contract. A crucial part of ethical theory will be to discern a basis for adopting some particular common goal-scale. This planning question is one that I haven't yet addressed. In particular, I haven't derived, from Harsanyi's second welfare theorem, that the overall good adds up everyone's individual good. I am not even assuming, at this point in the argument, that there's any sense to be made of talk of a person's individual good. Indeed from the austere materials I am allowing myself, I won't be able to derive such a conclusion. Decision-theoretic requirements of coherence in action won't by themselves entail that the common goal for each of us to pursue, in living together on a basis of mutual respect, adds up, in any sense, the good of each of us. Perhaps the overall good is formed in this way, but I won't be able to demonstrate that it is.

Here, though, is something that does follow from requirements of coherence. Take any consideration that weighs into the overall good. For all we have said, some of these considerations may concern no one in particular. Perhaps, as part of the social contract, we are to promote diversity of species on the planet. It is to count in favor of an action on the part of anyone, we might agree, that the action would promote species diversity. (I'm not discussing here whether species diversity indeed is something to promote for its own sake, just saying that coherence requirements don't rule this out.) Such a common goal, we can say, is *impersonal,* as opposed to *person-based.* With other goals that we are to take up in common, the grounds for doing so involve, in one way or another, an individual. They are considerations for the rest of us to weigh, under the social contract, because of the way their relation to that person gives her reason to want us to weigh them. Suffering presumably has this status: Your suffering pertains to you, and it is because you have reason to want not to suffer and so to want the social contract to work against your suffering that the social contract will tell everyone to want you not to suffer. (More precisely, it will tell everyone to treat the fact that you would suffer if something were done as weighing against doing it.) Now suffering is bad for a person if anything is, but other things that people tend to want have a status that is less clear. Prestige, honor, recognition after death, integrity, family thriving—these things are puzzling. If, though, the social contract tells us to give intrinsic weight to any of these, the grounds will presumably be person-based.

Suppose, then, a consideration has ethical import; the social contract tells us each to weigh it. We can ask whether the import is person-based or impersonal. Coherence doesn't demand that it must be person-based, for anything we have established, but if it is person-based, that gives the consideration a status worth singling out. A *person-based* consideration we can define as a consideration pertaining to some specific person that has moral weight because of how it pertains to him, and because of how the way it pertains to him gives him, in particular, reason to want it fostered by the social contract.

It is probably best, at this point, not to speak of a person's "good" but of his *interests*. (Scanlon adopts this usage.[4]) Our question now, after all, is not directly what to want in life for one's own sake, but what to include in the social contract, what considerations to agree to give weight to. The argument I have given doesn't establish that the person-based considerations to promote under the social contract must count as aspects of the person's "good" as we normally use the term. One interpretation we might now give to talk of a person's "interests" is this: a person's interests consist of those things that are of ethical import because, in this sense, they are *based* in him.

Trivially, any consideration that bears on the overall good is person-based or not; if not, it counts as impersonal. Suppose, then, there are no impersonal goods, that every consideration that the ideal social contract tells us to take into account is person-based. Will it follow that the overall good is the sum of individuals' interests? To establish this, we need one further assumption: that the common goal-scale that the contract prescribes—the scale that measures the overall good—sums up the weights of a set of considerations. Given this, since each consideration must either be person-based or impersonal and none of them are impersonal, they must all be person-based. The overall good, then, is measured on a scale that adds up the weights of person-based considerations—which is to say, of individuals' interests. Now I find it hard to see how a coherent goal-scale can have any rationale other than that it sums up the weight of a set of considerations. I don't know how to establish definitively that it must, but in the rest of what I say in this lecture, I'll assume that it must. If it does, the argument I have given shows that the overall good is composed of the interests of individuals.

All this assumed that there are no impersonal goods. Suppose instead that there are such goods. (Pick your favorite candidate; my example was species diversity.) Then by the same argument (with the same additional assumption), the overall good is composed of individual interests plus whatever impersonal goods the ideal social contract would include.

In either case, then, the social contract will tell us each to adopt a common goal-scale, and this goal-scale will be the resultant of our individual interests—along with, conceivably, certain impersonal goods.

What Is in a Person's Interests?

Consider three questions: (a) Is there such a thing as a person's interests? (b) If so, what are they? (c) Will the ideal social contract tell us each to pursue the sum of individuals' interests? I have been asking what these questions mean, and the meaning that we can give to talk of a person's "interests" on the basis of what I have been saying is this: a person's interests consist in whatever has moral weight because of how it pertains to her and how the way it pertains to her gives her in particular reason to want it fostered by the social contract. The three questions, as I'll interpret them, are all planning questions, questions of how to live with others. Harsanyi's second welfare theorem determines answers to transformed questions (a) and (c). It determines answers, that is, supposing that there is a basis for living with each other that no one could reasonably reject. This way of living together—the ideal social contract—is for each of us to adopt the same goal-scale, a scale that somehow accommodates things each of us has reason to want. Whatever this scale measures I call the overall good, and the way it is composed settles what counts as a person's interests. Thus (a) there is such a thing as a person's interests, and (c) the ideal social contract says to pursue the overall good, composed of the interests of all people plus, conceivably, of impersonal goods. (This assumes, remember, that the overall good is a resultant of considerations.)

That leaves question (b). What is in a person's interests? I have said that this is a planning question. It is roughly the question of what to count in the social contract. I haven't, though, addressed this question. It is one of the questions in ethics that I would like most to answer, but not a question that I aspired to answer in these lectures. I have been interpreting the question and asking what form a coherent answer must take. Trying to answer the question must lead to almost all the questions that ethical inquiry addresses.

Let me speak briefly about this question, though. Hedonic goods obviously enter in: happiness, enjoying what one does and getting satisfaction from it, freedom from suffering, positive "hedonic tone," and the like. One chief puzzle, debated over the years, concerns what used to be called "ideal" goods. G. E. Moore listed as the greatest goods "organic wholes" involving pleasures of friendship and pleasures of contemplating beauty.[5] These things involve pleasure and more: roughly, that one derives pleasure, in characteristic ways, from genuine friendship and genuine beauty. James Griffin ventures a list of prudential values beyond enjoyment as accomplishment, understanding, deep personal relations, and components of human existence such as autonomy, basic capabilities, and liberty.[6] One question, widely debated, is whether these really are things to want for their own sakes. Or are they instead things to want just because they reliably go with the greatest of pleasures?

Either way, they are things to want in life and things to want our social arrangements to foster. Do they count intrinsically, though, as parts of what the overall good consists in? If they are worth wanting for their own sake, and if the ideal social contract tells us each to advance some common overall good, aren't these things worth counting among the things we agree to foster jointly?

Rawls himself thought not. He thought that not even enjoyment and freedom from suffering would figure among the "primary social goods" used to assess possible social arrangements. Some arguments against maximizing the total pleasure or happiness of people strike me as bad. (Nozick worried about "utility monsters" who make themselves highly sensitive to income level and the like, so that their needs for income will count more heavily under the social contract, and they will be awarded the lion's share of resources.[7] But a wise implementation of the social contract will heed incentive effects and not reward a person's setting himself up to suffer unless rich. He may threaten to hold his breath until given a million dollars, but a wise system won't respond even if the threat is credible.) Other arguments for Rawls's position, though, call for careful thought; they concern what people's interests are and how they can be compared. An interrelated problem is how people are to live together on a basis of mutual respect when they disagree fundamentally about what to want in life and on facts that bear on how to pursue it. I'll try to lay out these problems within the metaethical framework that I have sketched in these lectures.

Interpersonal Comparisons and Reasonable Disagreement

Here is a first problem, serious but solvable: Begin with the question of what to want from a social contract on *self-based* grounds. By these I'll mean grounds that, because of how they pertain to oneself in particular, give one reason to want the social contract to accord them weight. What fundamentally self-based grounds there are is a planning question, and intelligible enough. What, then, constitute a person's interests? An interest of his, recall, we define as a consideration pertaining to him that the ideal social contract accords weight because of how it pertains to him, and because of how the way it pertains to him gives him, in particular, reason to want it fostered by the social contract. If the social contract is made for him and the rest of humanity, then it may seem that his interests in this sense are just the things for him to want from the social contract on self-based grounds.

How, though, if that is so, are we to compare the strengths of interests of different people? How is the social contract to trade off their interests against each other, when those interests can't all jointly be catered to? A person's interests may well depend on his personal characteristics, since what to want from a social contract might differ from person to person, in a way that depends on those characteristics. In saying this we must keep in mind the difference between two related questions: the psychological question of what the person *does* want, and the planning question of what *to* want in case one is that person with that person's characteristics. Characteristics in which we differ may well matter for both, but here, remember, our question is what *to* want. We differ in what gives us a sense of meaning and fulfillment in our lives, we differ in our ideals for ourselves, and so there may be different things to want in case one is like you and in case one is like me—or things to want in different strengths. You thrive on controversy, perhaps, and I on dogma, and we can protect my sensibilities or give scope to your free tongue and spirit. Protection is something to want in case one is like me, imagine, and scope in case one is like you. How compare, then, the urgency of protecting me and of giving you scope, when we can't do both? That is the first problem.

So posed, the problem seems solvable, in somewhat the way that Harsanyi envisaged.[8] I can distinguish what to want from the social contract in case one is like you and what to want from it in case one is like me. I can compare how strongly to want things by facing the hypothetical planning questions of what to prefer if one is equally likely to be like you or like me, and choosing between being provided for in the one case and in the other. This gives us a comparison of person-based interests, and a person could reasonably reject, it seems to me, having his interests weighed at less than what this comparison indicates.

Rawls's aim, though, was to find a basis for living on a basis of mutual respect that suits people who disagree fundamentally on what to want in life. My discussion so far has assumed that planning questions like these have right answers, and that the terms of the ideal social contract can depend on what these right answers are. Whether planning questions like these do have right answers, answers that are interpersonally valid, is a difficult issue that I won't here try to address. (I struggle with this in both my books.[9]) Even if these questions do have right answers, though, we surely don't agree on them. Rawls's problem, couched in my terms, was how to live together on a basis of mutual respect in the face of perennial, fundamental disagreement on basic questions of planning and of fact. We are back to Ida who wants a big funeral and Jay who thinks that a big funeral is not a thing to want for its own sake even if one is like Ida. How can they live together in mutual respect, on a basis that neither would reject even if she had the power to force an alternative on the other?

Rawls proposed marking off a range of answers to basic questions of planning and of fact as "reasonable." His question was not the general one of how to live together with others on a basis of mutual respect in the face of any fundamental, perennial disagreement whatsoever. Rather, it was how to do so when others' views, even if mistaken, are reasonable. As for what counts as "reasonable," that must amount to a planning question. To treat a view as reasonable in this sense, we might try saying, is to be willing to accommodate it. It is to want to live with those who hold the view on a basis that they can accept, with a rationale that prescinds from questions on which they don't share the truth as one sees it. It is to prefer this to the alternative of imposing a social order on them—even for the case of having the power to suppress them.

This lecture has centered on a Harsanyi-like argument that what's up for negotiation in arranging a social contract is what to count as a person's interests—and possibly what to count as impersonal goods. To be coherent, I argued, a social contract must specify a single goal-scale for us each to make his own. How, then, if the argument I gave is good, does it bear on Rawls's project? Even if the argument is good, it may still be that some people won't accept it, even when offered careful explanations. It may nevertheless be best to undertake to live with them on some basis that, given their views, they will accept. If "reasonable" views are ones to be willing to accommodate in a scheme of voluntary social cooperation, this means that even if everyone ought to accept the arguments I have given, rejecting them may count as reasonable. Moreover, suppose that everyone does accept the Harsanyi-like argument that I gave. Still, even if we all accept the same conception of a person's interests and all accept that we each are to advance the combined interests of everyone, we may disagree fundamentally on the facts that bear on how to do this. What we may still all be able to agree on, in that case, is a basic structure of society, a way to proceed in face of our disagreements—even though none of us thinks that it is the structure that most fosters the totality of people's interests.

The arguments I have given, then, speak to Rawls's problem only in special circumstances, circumstances where there is more agreement on what matters in life than Rawls envisaged. My arguments don't tell us how Ida and Jay are to live in a scheme of voluntary social cooperation and mutual respect when they can't agree on the worth that a big funeral would have for Ida once she was dead. Perhaps the two can agree to count a big funeral as in one's interests if one cared when alive and not if one didn't. Perhaps if they *can* so agree, then whoever is right on the worth of funerals, they each *ought* to so agree. Probably they ought to agree on a scheme much like the one that Rawls advocates, establishing a basic social structure that gives both of them good prospects for multipurpose means like income and opportunities. Ida can then have her funeral if she or others want to bear the costs. No ethical conclusions along lines like these follow from anything I have said, and nothing I have said tells us how to choose among alternative economic schemes that share these overall features. We are left with the problem of how to compare different people's interests.

I won't finish these lectures with a solution to Rawls's problem— I'd love to, but I can't. Rawls himself, in my judgment, didn't come up with a compelling solution, and neither has anyone else. What terms of social cooperation are worth accepting when we disagree fundamentally on basic questions of fact and value must depend, I would think, on many questions of fact, psychological and sociological, and on difficult questions of what to prefer in light of those facts. What is the range of views to be reconciled, in what numbers? What are the effects of forcing people on various matters against their convictions? How are we to deal with these facts; what attitudes are we to have toward the people with whom we disagree? It would be surprising if some game-theoretic scheme held a straightforward answer to such questions—though game-theoretic insights may be highly relevant.

Through all this indeterminate discussion of Rawls's project, though, the force of the Harsanyi-like result of this lecture remains. Any social contract will be self-frustrating unless it takes a certain utilitarian-like form: agreeing to maximize prospects on some common goal-scale. Otherwise, there will be a possible alternative social arrangement that, for each person, offers better prospects in terms of what that person is trying to accomplish. The lesson of the canoe examples survives. That leaves the question of how the common goal-scale of the ideal social contract is to be set. What if we disagreed fundamentally on the importance of saving our children or on how to assess the facts that bear on how best to save them? Confronted with the problem that Rawls sets, I have found no compelling, tractable answer. The finding remains, though, that without such a common-goal scale, our social arrangements are jointly self-frustrating.

Harsanyi and Beyond

If a social arrangement is jointly self-frustrating, I have been supposing, then anyone could reasonably reject it. Some alternative to it, after all, is better with respect to each person—better, that is to say, as reckoned in terms of the values that this very arrangement tells her to promote. Getting further in our inquiry, though, would require more examination of this claim: If a social arrangement is jointly self-frustrating, does that truly make it reasonable to reject the arrangement? Progress would also require careful scrutiny of other assumptions I invoked. Do those assumptions apply to our actual circumstances? Or do they at least apply to circumstances that are relevant to moral argument? What is the upshot when they don't?

Recall how my argument went. The conclusion was that a social contract must establish a common goal-scale for all of us to advance—on pain of being jointly self-frustrating. Start first with an individual: For him, sheer coherence in action requires pursuing some goal-scale or other; he will act as if he were maximizing prospects as reckoned by that scale. This is the upshot of arguments by Hammond and others; in these lectures I accepted those arguments with little scrutiny. Turn now to society and the social contract. If each individual pursues a distinct goal-scale—favoring, say, his own children or his own integrity—the result, it turns out, must be collectively self-frustrating. It will be self-frustrating in this sense: There will be an alternative goal-scale that we all might have pursued in common, thereby achieving prospects that are better on each person's goal-scale. This is the Harsanyi-like result that I have been exploring.

What rationale, I next asked, could there be for agreeing to a social contract with this blemish? Couldn't any of us reasonably reject such a self-frustrating social contract? For each of us, after all, what it tells him to pursue is better attained, in prospect, by the same alternative social contract, an alternative that hands us a common array of goals to pursue. This result goes part way to what utilitarians have always claimed, and it is at odds with many of our intuitive judgments—as with the canoe rescue case of Jeske and Fumerton. If one's children are so greatly worth saving, the point is, why agree to less than best prospects for their being saved?

I can't claim, though, that such a challenge is unanswerable. Indeed many cogent answers have been explored by ethical theorists. The argument depends, of course, on supposing that there is a form of social cooperation that no one could reasonably reject. This amounts to supposing that ethics, in a contractarian vein, is possible. I have chiefly assumed as well, implicitly, that we have an agreed basis for judgments of non-ethical fact, a basis that lets us speak of "prospects" as reckoned by some particular goal-scale. I have assumed moreover that we would each implement whatever we agreed to, and implement it costlessly and with perfect rationality—and that we all know that we would. It was on these assumptions at least that I based my conclusions, and further inquiry demands seeing how those assumptions should be relaxed and what the upshot then is.

Compliance and its costs raise acute problems, in life and in moral theory. A social ethos never gets perfect compliance, and only costly efforts could achieve even partial compliance. Utilitarians have long faced this problem; they have proposed solutions for it and debated the adequacy of those solutions.[10] Rule-utilitarianism and other forms of indirect utilitarianism distinguish a background rationale for morality, which is utilitarian, with morality made for humanity, from the moral code for a society that the rationale supports. The moral code may invoke a notion of individuals' interests or their good and still not tell each of us to promote the total good or interest of all of us—even if the background rationale for the code is to promote the totality of people's "interests" in another sense of the term. There may well be, then, an indirect rationale for the sort of limited notion of interests that Rawls and Scanlon advocate, and for a moral code that tells us to heed not only people's interests but their rights and their autonomy. Rawls too distinguishes a background rationale from the principles of justice that are to govern the basic structure of society, and he too expects only partial compliance.[11] A contractarian like Rawls must worry about partial compliance for a further reason that I have mentioned: His basic rationale for heeding morality is reciprocity, and with partial compliance, though there's something to reciprocate, there's less than there might be. In brief, no social contract we could want will draw full compliance, and the upshot is a central problem for ethical theory.

My discussion has left out much else that needs study, including much that is already receiving valuable treatment in the literature of moral philosophy. Among other things, I have said nothing about a person's right to make his own mistakes, about possible conflicts between respect for his autonomy and concern for his welfare. I think that much could be said about this and other matters within the kind of framework that Harsanyi sets up, but I have not myself been doing the work in these lectures.

The lesson I draw from Harsanyi, then, is crucial but limited. Any ethic that lets us pursue basically different purposes faces a challenge. The challenge does not end discussion, but it should inform any broad inquiry into ethical theory. Is it ethically permissible for any of us to give special heed to our own special concerns and our own particular responsibilities? Doubtless yes, but why? Why shouldn't any such claim be rejected as self-frustrating? We haven't established that an ethical theorist who makes such a claim has no answer, but he does owe us one. What is the point of moral strictures? If the background rationale for the strictures isn't some aim we could have in common to accommodate our various individual ends, can the rationale be fully coherent?

Questions of ethics are, in effect, planning questions, I started out saying. They are questions of how to live with other people who face like questions. I have been addressing a range of fundamental questions of ethical theory as planning questions. The way to live with other people if one can, I took it, is on a voluntary basis that no one could reasonably reject. In accepting such an ideal for living together, I had to rely on intuitions on how to want to live with others. A crucial range of ethical puzzles then became questions of what to want from a social contract, and what sort of social contract to respect if it is in force. Requirements of coherence on plans, I began to argue, generate restrictions on the kind of social contract that no one could reasonably reject.

The demands of coherence in our ethical thinking can be powerful, and they sometimes run counter to strong intuitions. Amartya Sen and Bernard Williams published, almost two decades ago, a collection of articles that included both a lucid summary by Harsanyi of his ethical thinking and Scanlon's own initial exposition of his "contractualism." The editors entitled their collection *Utilitarianism and Beyond*. The title was apt in a way: We do still need to get beyond the point that ethical theory has reached. To do so, though, we can't move beyond utilitarianism and drop it. We must still heed the force of the kinds of considerations that Harsanyi raised. Any moral vision that doesn't specify a common goal-scale as a basis of its rationale must explain why it doesn't fall in the face of a Harsanyi-like result. We can forge beyond Harsanyi only by keeping careful track of what he showed.

Notes

1. Kant, *Groundwork* (1785). Hare, in "Could Kant Have Been a Utilitarian?" (1993), argues that, although Kant was convinced

that his system yielded the pietistic morality of ordinary people of good will, his system cannot be made to yield the results he wanted except by making unsupportable and *ad hoc* moves. Most other recent and current Kantians think that a Kantian rationale can be given for a morality that departs fundamentally from utilitarianism.

2. We could instead use the term 'utility scale' for what I am calling a 'goal-scale,' and thus latch onto one of the meanings that highly theoretical economists and decision theorists have for the term 'utility': a scale representing, in a canonical way, how a person is disposed to make his decisions. The term 'my utility,' though, also suggests my good or my interest, and we must sharply distinguish the scale I adopt under the terms of the social contract to guide my choices from my own good or my own interests, which the social contract accommodates.

3. For a more precise formulation, see the appendix.

4. Scanlon uses the term 'interests' in this way; see, for instance, *What We Owe* (1998), p. 136.

5. Moore, *Principia Ethica* (1903). He didn't think these to be person-based goods in my sense; he treated all goods as impersonal. I take this to be far from the spirit of contractarianism, the kind of moral vision that I pursue in these lectures.

6. Griffin, *Well-Being* (1986), p. 67. His list is of course meant as rough and tentative.

7. Nozick, *Anarchy, State, and Utopia* (1973), p. 41. My reply here concerns a threat to suffer terribly if one isn't given resources. It is true that if a person can achieve extraordinary happiness with additional money and not otherwise, utilitarianism will treat it as urgent for him to have the money. But wealth beyond dreams, we find, doesn't make for happiness beyond dreams; we can't make ourselves into "utility monsters" of this kind.

8. Harsanyi, "Cardinal Welfare" (1955).

9. *Wise Choices* (1990), pp. 153–203, and *Thinking How to Live* (2003), pp. 268–87.

10. Sidgwick confronts these problems and sticks with a direct utilitarianism. Brandt develops a form of rule utilitarianism in "Toward a Credible" (1963), "Some Merits" (1967), and *A Theory*

(1979). Harsanyi, in "Morality" (1977), endorsed Brandt's rule utilitarianism. Hare, in *Moral Thinking* (1981), distinguishes questions on two levels, the "critical" and the "intuitive." He argues that at the critical level, only act-utilitarianism fits the logic of moral thinking, whereas at the intuitive level of thinking we should accept precepts that are not directly utilitarian.

11. By his background rationale, I mean his specification of the "original position" and his arguments that the test of principles of justice is what would be chosen in the original position as he specifies it. Roughly, in *Theory of Justice*, the rationale for principles of justice is that we would have chosen them in a fair situation to govern the basic structure of society. In subsequent work, he expands on the "Kantian interpretation" of his theory and stresses that the rationale involves expressing our nature as free and rational beings. Parties in the original position expect partial compliance in that, although they know that the principles they choose will govern the basic structure of their society and be widely accepted, they do not expect unanimous acceptance of the principles or invariable conformity to them. They must provide for education and enforcement and choose principles that, once implemented, would continue to be widely accepted and adhered to.

Appendix: The Harsanyi-like Result

ALLAN GIBBARD

The "Harsanyi-like result" that I rely on in the third lecture is just the following. It is a form of argument familiar to economic theorists, although the niceties of just when it holds require some care. Start with all the possible policies for action that each person could adopt. A policy—or *strategy*, as I'll say to fit game-theoretic terminology—assigns an action to each informational state that one might be in. For each person, some conceivable strategies are feasible for him and others are not. Call an assignment of a strategy to each person a *strategy profile*. A strategy profile is feasible just in case each person's strategy for that profile is feasible for him. Assume a unique prior subjective probability measure that everyone shares at the start and then updates with new information. Then we can speak of the *prospect* that a strategy profile presents; it assigns to each possible outcome the probability that outcome would have if each person acted on his strategy for that profile.

Let each person have a goal-scale. Any prospect has an expected value on a given person's goal-scale; call this the *prospective value to* him of that prospect. For a given prospect, call the assignment to each person of the prospective value to him of that prospect the *value profile* of that prospect. For any strategy profile, we can thus speak of the value profile of the prospect that the strategy presents; call this the value profile *yielded* by strategy profile.

A value profile is *feasible* if it is yielded by some feasible strategy profile. In that case, it is attainable by perfect conformity to some possible social contract—namely, the social contract that tells each person to adopt the strategy assigned him by that strategy profile. The *feasible set* of value profiles is the set of feasible value profiles. For the case of two people, we can represent any value profile on paper by its Cartesian coordinates, and so we can represent the feasible set of value profiles by a set of points. A possible example is shown in Figure A1. A feasible value profile is *non-dominated* iff no other feasible value profile has a higher value on one person's goal-scale without having a lower value on someone else's.

Suppose first that set of feasible value profiles is strictly convex. The non-dominated feasible value profiles then lie on the frontier of this convex set. Each, then, lies maximally in one direction—and this amounts to saying that there is a possible goal-scale on which it is maximal. (Draw a tangent to the feasible set at that point; the

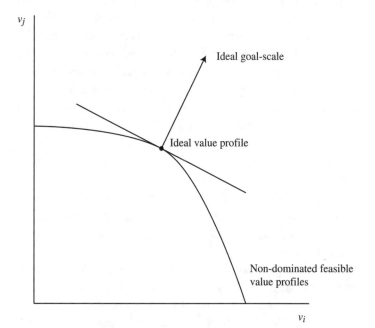

Figure A1

goal-scale is a vector that points outward perpendicular to this tangent.) Take, then, any non-dominated feasible value profile, and suppose that the ideal social contract would tell each to adopt a strategy that, jointly, yields this value profile. Call this the *ideal value profile*, and call this goal-scale the *ideal goal scale*. Among feasible value profiles, the ideal value profile comes out highest on the ideal goal-scale. (In case the feasible set is convex but not strictly, then perhaps more than one value profile will have this property.[1])

We still might ask whether individuals can jointly reach this ideal value profile by each acting always to maximize prospects as reckoned by the ideal goal-scale. To this question the answer is no: As utilitarians have long realized, individually rational utilitarians may fail to coordinate and hence achieve an outcome that is suboptimal. (In my dissertation, my first example was a village of act-utilitarians threatened with destruction by a giant boulder; each villager rescues as many children and possessions as possible, each doing the best he can given what others are disposed to do. Jointly, though, they might have pushed the boulder harmlessly down the other side of the hill.)

The result I appeal to is rather this: In abiding by the ideal social contract, each person acts always to produce prospects that are maximal on the ideal goal-scale. Or at least this is so under certain conditions, which I will sketch. This is an application of the theorem originally about utilitarianism. Take a community of perfect act-utilitarians, and suppose first that they could make binding any agreement they chose. Call an agreement that they would then make *optimal*. The theorem is that if an agreement is optimal, and if it is common knowledge that they will each keep that agreement, then each will keep the agreement even if it has not been made binding.[2] The theorem applies to people disposed always to act to maximize prospects on a common goal-scale, whether or not that goal-scale is in any sense utilitarian. The conditions are the following: (1) value as reckoned by the goal-scale stems from coordination only, so that no value or disvalue stems from anticipation, teaching, or resources being expended on calculation; (2) full agreement in subjective probabilities when the agreement is made; (3) full memory as strategies are acted on.

Matters are more complex if we drop the assumption that the feasible set is convex. Then it may be that a non-dominated feasible value profile is maximal among feasible value profiles on no goal-scale, as shown in figure A2. If, though, any probability mixture of feasible strategy profiles is feasible, then the set of feasible value profiles will be convex.

What if parties don't all agree in their prior subjective probabilities—though each is still perfectly coherent and each counts as

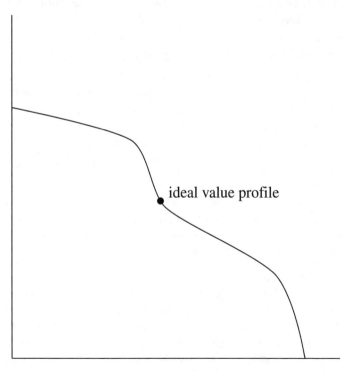

ideal value profile

Figure A2

reasonable? The assumption that people do agree in their subjective probabilities at the time of making the agreement is crucial to the theorem about act-utilitarian agreements that I am reinterpreting, and Broome has a result that is discouraging on this score.[3] The upshot of Broome's result in the present framework and what the consequences are for moral theory I leave for further inquiry.

Another question this Harsanyi-like result raises is what work the social coherence assumption was doing in the second Harsanyi theorem in the first place. I have argued that the ideal social contract is non-dominated, and it follows from this and convexity that there is a goal-scale on which it maximizes prospects. Coherence is partly a matter of ordering, and the import of a preference ordering lies in how it constrains what's optimal as the feasible set changes. I have considered only a fixed feasible set of prospects. We can ask, then, whether the social contracts that are ideal for different possible circumstances—the ones that, given those circumstances, no one could reasonably reject—all maximize the same goal-scale. Many contractarians will answer no.[4] If this points to an ethos of "To each according to his bargaining position," we may however conclude that it is reasonable to reject such a basis for free, unforced agreement on the basic structure of society.

This leads to difficult questions about contractarianism. Do the principles that no one could reasonably reject change as new information unfolds, information about such things as our respective social positions, needs, abilities, and the like that affect our bargaining positions? If so, it will be hard to interpret Scanlon's test: We need principles that no one could reasonably reject, but reject at what point? If not, then we can consider a highly prospective standpoint for the acceptance or rejection of principles, and this may look a lot like Rawls's original position or Harsanyi's ethical standpoint. I won't, however, investigate these issues further here.

Notes

1. Gibbard, *Utilitarianisms and Coordination* (1971).

2. Gibbard, "Act-Utilitarian Agreements" (1978), pp. 112–18; also in *Utilitarianisms and Coordination* (1971), pp. 186–93. The theorem was proved only for finite models.

3. Broome, *Weighing Goods* (1991), pp. 152–54.

4. Gauthier, *Morals by Agreement* (1991), and Binmore, *Playing Fair* (1994), are examples.

Comments

Normative Thinking and Planning, Individual and Shared: Reflections on Allan Gibbard's Tanner Lectures

Michael Bratman

There is thinking, conducted by a single person, about how to live. And there is thinking together—a kind of "language infused" (15) shared activity—about how to live together. In the first of these fascinating and deeply probing Tanner Lectures, Allan Gibbard is concerned with both of these phenomena and with how they interact.

Begin with some of the main views presented in this lecture. We face questions of what to do and why. That we face these questions is a fact about the kind of beings in the natural world that we are. However, a "full and adequate naturalistic, biological story" will not, Gibbard avers, "contain any fact" that our answers to these questions of what to do and why are "right or not" (18). Here Gibbard agrees with G. E. Moore. Gibbard also eschews appeal to non-natural facts about what we ought to do, facts that are not part of the naturalistic story. Here Gibbard disagrees with Moore. Nevertheless, as Gibbard sees it, our answers to these practical questions do constitute a kind of judgment. Our judgments about what to do are, to a first approximation, *plans* about what to do. And judgments about what to do are the basic case of judgments about what one *ought* to do: "*ought* thoughts are like plans" (19). To make a practical normative judgment—a judgment about what someone ought to do or has reason to do—is, at bottom, to plan.

This may sound jarring. Gibbard's talk of plans is not just talk of plan-like contents. A recipe is a plan-like content, a content one might think about without planning to act on. Talk of plans here is talk, rather, of attitudes of planning to. Such planning attitudes, we might say, aim at changing the world, at making the world fit them; but judgments aim at fitting the world. While it is difficult to know exactly how to interpret such talk of an aim of an attitude, it does seem we are here getting at a fairly basic difference between judgments and plan-type attitudes. As is frequently said, judgments and plans have different "directions of fit." So how can plans *be* judgments?

Well, Gibbard would acknowledge some such distinction, at least initially, between ordinary empirical beliefs about the natural world and attitudes of planning to act. His view is that nevertheless an important sub-set of these planning attitudes behaves in a sufficiently belief-like way to count as judgment. Given the temporal extension of our thought and action, an agent needs to some extent to trust her earlier plans in her later planning, just as she needs to trust her earlier beliefs (26): Both planning and belief involve a kind of cross-temporal self-trust. And just as beliefs are subject to constraints of consistency and coherence, so, according to Gibbard, are one's planning attitudes. Given Gibbard's apparent identification of planning to A with strictly preferring A to its alternatives, these constraints are to some extent specified in formal decision theory; and, as the Zeckhauser Russian roulette example is intended to show, they can lead to striking results. Further, just as one's beliefs are subject to pressure toward agglomeration—toward putting them together into an overall view of the world—the various planning attitudes of an agent are subject to pressure toward constituting at least a part of a "complete contingency plan for living" (30). We can then go on to ask which possibilities are, and which are not, consistent with one's overall plans, just as we can ask which possibilities are, and which are not, consistent with one's set of beliefs; "and judgments get their content from what they are consistent with and what not" (30). All this is offered in support of the idea that we can see at least certain plans as sufficiently belief-like to count as judgments.

What about my judgment that *someone else* ought to act in a certain way in a certain circumstance? This judgment cannot simply be my planning so to act, since I know that I am not that person in that circumstance. On Gibbard's view, my judgment is, rather, a contingency plan for what to do were I that person in that circumstance. I can have such a contingency plan even for circumstances in which, as I know, I will never be. In Gibbard's example, I can have a plan for what to do were I Caesar at the Rubicon; and my thought about what Caesar ought to have done involves such a contingency plan.

What about specifically *moral* judgment? On the theory, moral ought judgments are, to a first approximation, plans about "what moral sentiments to have." They are, in particular, plans about "what to resent people for doing and what to feel guilty for doing" (16)—where these emotions of resentment and guilt play a central role in our "social world" (15).

What about judgments not directly of what one ought to do, but of what there is *reason* to do? Well, we not only plan what to do, we plan what is to count, and in what ways, in our deliberation about what to do. We have plans about weights in deliberation—where, to avoid circularity in the account of the idea of a reason, we understand deliberation as a mental activity that is characterized, in a basic case, without appeal to that idea of a reason.[1] Judgments about reasons are plans about what to weigh in deliberation.

This gives us a way of understanding the idea of an *intuition*, a way of understanding this idea without appealing to some special "power to apprehend" something non-natural (13). Some plans about what to weigh are basic in the sense that, on reflection, we do not support them by appeal to yet a further plan about weights.

Such a basic plan about weights amounts to "an intuition about why to do things" (22). In that sense, we ground our normative thinking in intuition. Such an intuition is a normative judgment. It is not just a tendency to give weight to some consideration—avoidance of suffering, say; it involves a *plan to* give such weight. And we can express its content as: Such and such is a reason to act in certain ways.

We also have plans about when—under what conditions—to *trust* our planning, and so when to trust our ought judgments. We might plan to trust our planning under, say, conditions of full information vividly presented. Such plans for trusting planning are judgments about what conditions for planning are "ideal." Given such a judgment about what are ideal conditions—that is, a plan for trusting planning in those conditions—I can ask: If I were in those ideal conditions, what would I judge I ought to do in a certain circumstance? What, for example, would I, in ideal conditions, judge I ought to do if I were one of the fathers in the example Gibbard sketches? If I determine that I would, in those ideal conditions, judge that I ought to save my own child, then if I follow through on my plan to trust judgments made in those ideal conditions, I arrive at the judgment that I ought to save my own child— where that judgment involves a plan so to act in this scenario. So I can reason to an ought conclusion from a factual statement about what I would judge in certain ideal conditions, but only because in the background is a plan to trust judgments made in those ideal conditions. My ought judgment is not reducible simply to a naturalistic claim in "interpreted psychology" (22).

As Gibbard notes in his 2003 book,[2] this leaves open the possibility that I think that what *I* would judge in ideal conditions differs from what *you* would judge in ideal conditions. In such a case, I think that there is no judgment *we* would reach in ideal conditions, that we are, in this respect, at an "impasse." I will return to this possibility at the end.

This planning theory of normative judgment requires a further refinement. We sometimes decide between options neither of which we think strictly superior to the other. Perhaps I think two routes from Palo Alto to Berkeley are equally desirable. Or perhaps, as in Sartre's famous case, I must choose between staying home with my ill mother and fighting for the Free French, and I think the conflicting considerations are incomparable[3] and that neither option is superior to the other. In each case, we can suppose, I reach a decision, and so there is one option I plan to perform. But I do not think I *ought* to do specifically what I plan to do. What I think is only that I ought to perform one or the other of the options. So planning to act does not ensure thinking I ought so to act.

This leads to a complexity in Gibbard's theory. To think an act *okay*, Gibbard says, is to "rule out preferring any alternative" (20). To think one *ought* to act is to think it is okay so to act, and not okay not to. What is it to "rule out" a preference? Well, given Gibbard's approach, it seems that the idea is that to rule out a preference is to *plan* not to prefer.[4] Thinking it okay to A is to plan not to prefer A's alternatives to A itself. In our first example, then, I plan not to prefer route #1 over route #2; and I also plan not to prefer route #2 over route #1: I think each route okay. Thinking I ought to A is, at least to a first approximation, to plan not to prefer A's alternatives to A itself, and to plan to prefer A to its alternatives. And, I take it, Gibbard is assuming that if I plan to prefer A to its alternatives, I thereby plan to A—so this new story of thinking I ought to A, as a complex plan to prefer, meshes with the original story of thinking I ought to A, as a plan to act; but the new story aims to work better for cases of "ties" and thinking only that an option is okay.

Let me now briefly raise some questions. Some touch on issues Gibbard has discussed elsewhere. My aim is to create a context in which he can tell us more.

First, what should we say about cases of thinking one ought to A and yet, out of weakness of will, planning instead to do something else? Perhaps I think I ought to limit myself to one glass of wine, yet I give in to temptation and drink a second glass. It seems that, sad to say, my thought that I ought to stick with one glass fails to involve my planning to stick with one glass.[5]

Second, it is central to Gibbard's idea that plans are belief-like that they are subject to a constraint of agglomeration and consistency: One's various plans need to be such that they can all "be realized in a complete contingency plan for living" (30). But why exactly are these plans subject to this constraint? After all, intrinsic desires are not subject to such a constraint: I might well intrinsically desire each of two different things without intrinsically desiring— or even believing to be possible in the circumstances—their joint realization. Further, as Gibbard emphasizes, some of the plans needed for his theory of normative thinking "are wild contingency plans that I'll never be in a position to carry out anyway" (29). Why should all such "wild contingency plans" be subject to agglomeration into a single "complete" plan?

Gibbard indicates that he does not here "seriously" enter into debates about "whether the conditions on plans that [standard decision-theoretic] arguments invoke are genuinely requirements of coherence" (59). But something needs to be said at least about the pressure for plan agglomeration, since in its absence the parallel with belief seems a non-starter. And Gibbard does briefly engage this matter at the end of the first lecture. So let us reflect on what such a theory might say.

In the case of belief, we can ground a demand for agglomeration and consistency in the connection between belief and truth. But even if in the end we can talk of plans as being true or false, we cannot use that idea at this point in the argument. As Gibbard says, "we don't start our treatment with talk of truth and falsehood and help ourselves to these notions in our initial theorizing" (29). We need an account of the cited constraint on plans that appeals, at bottom, not to a connection between planning and truth, but to something else.

Is what is needed here a claim about the *reasons* we have to make our plans conform to this constraint, about why we *ought* to conform? Well, if this is how we initially proceed, we seem threatened with an odd circularity. After all, such a judgment about reasons would itself be a substantive normative judgment. On the planning theory of normative judgment, this judgment is itself a kind of plan. But this planning theory of normative judgment depends on the pressure to agglomerate plans, a pressure that purportedly parallels the pressure to agglomerate beliefs. If the source of that pressure is this very judgment that we have reason to—ought to—conform to the demand for agglomeration, we seem to be moving in a circle. This suggests that at the most basic level such a theory of normative thinking needs to look for a different kind of support for the agglomeration constraint on plans—which is not to deny that there are reasons for such conformity. But what might this be?[6]

Well, as Gibbard emphasizes, if one's plans significantly violated this constraint, we would not be able to assign them content in a way that parallels the assignment of content to beliefs. But we cannot appeal here to this point to explain why plans are subject to these constraints, for at this stage in the argument the issue is whether plans are indeed belief-like.

One idea here would be to appeal to the roles of plans in coordinating thought and action over time and socially. As we might try saying: Each plan aims not simply at making the world fit it, but at making the world fit it as an element in a coordinated realization of one's overall system of plans. Much of Gibbard's work emphasizes the *social* coordinating work of normative thinking;[7] and I take it he would also emphasize the *intra*personal coordinating work of planning. And I myself have tried to understand such constraints on plans and planning along some such lines.[8] So this is perhaps a convergence in our approaches to the nature of planning. We can wonder, however, whether the "wild contingency plans" that are endemic to Gibbard's theory of normative thinking really are part of a single coordinating system.[9] Is my plan for what to do were I Caesar at the Rubicon part of a single coordinating system that includes my more ordinary contingency plans—for example, my plan for what to do were I at the Hudson River?

Third, return to cases of "ties" and thinking okay. Suppose the boy in Sartre's case finds himself with a slight, felt preference for mom. But he still thinks the options involve incomparable considerations, and that neither option is, uniquely, what he ought to do. He thinks it okay to perform either option. But—in contrast with Gibbard's account—he does not plan not to prefer mom over the Free French; indeed, he continues slightly to prefer mom.

Perhaps we should put more theoretical weight on plans for weighing, rather than preferences over options and plans to act. On the theory, plans for weighing constitute judgments about reasons. When I think I ought to stop with one drink, my plans for weighing favor one drink over two, and I know this. Perhaps a theory like Gibbard's can say that my thought that I ought to stop with one drink expresses this known structural feature of my plans for weighing. And it can do that even if I plan to have a second drink—that plan is a plan for action, not a plan for weighing. Again, the boy in Sartre's case has, so far, plans for weighing that leave unsettled his decision between mom and the Free French, and he knows this. Perhaps a theory like Gibbard's can say that his thought that either is okay expresses this known structural feature of his plans for weighing; and this structural feature is compatible with his preference for mom, since a preference need not be a plan for weighing.[10]

Return now to the basic idea of identifying normative judgments with plans. If you judge that one ought to A in circumstance C, and I judge that one ought not to A in that circumstance, we are not merely differing, as we might if we have different tastes for flavors of ice cream: We are *disagreeing*. But if you plan to A in C whereas I plan to refrain from A in C, we are, it may seem, not disagreeing but just differing in what we each plan to do if in C. Will the features of plans already cited as supporting the idea that plans are judgment-like—pressures for consistency, coherence, agglomeration, and self-trust over time; assignment of content by appeal to what is consistent with one's overall plans—also explain why you and I may be disagreeing, not just differing, in plan? Well, so far these features of plans are individualistic: They explain, perhaps, why when I change my plans I am, in certain cases, disagreeing—and not merely differing—with my earlier self.[11] But it seems that we do not yet have the resources to explain why you and I may be disagreeing.

It is here, I take it, that Gibbard would appeal not simply to *my* thinking about how to live and to *your* thinking about how to live, but to *our jointly thinking together* about how to live. When I change my own plans over time, this can count as disagreement with my earlier self in part because, given the temporal extension of my thought and action, I see my earlier plans as having a defeasible claim on me now. In contrast, it is possible for me not to treat your ought thoughts as making any such claim on my ought thoughts. But insofar as we are engaged in thinking *together* about how to live, I will see your thoughts as making a claim on my thinking, a claim that is analogous to the claim of the thoughts of my past self. There is, then, pressure to keep track of the extent of agreement between us, just as there is pressure on me now to keep track of the extent of agreement between me now and me earlier. So, given that we are engaged in shared thinking about how to live, our differences in plan can constitute disagreements in plan. And I take it Gibbard would say that there are "selection pressures" (16) in favor of dispositions, on the part of a "highly social, linguistic species like ours" (30), to engage in such shared thinking. It is, then, the sociality of normative thinking—rather than independent facts (natural or non-natural) about oughts and reasons—that explains the nature of interpersonal normative disagreement as disagreement—and not merely difference—in plan.[12]

Let me close with a brief question about this. Suppose you think you are at an impasse with another person and for that reason opt out of shared thinking with that person about how to live. Can and should Gibbard's theory nevertheless make room for your thought that, despite this impasse, you ought to act in a certain way and that, in this normative judgment, you are disagreeing—and not merely differing—with that other person?[13]

Notes

1. See Allan Gibbard, *Thinking How to Live* (2003) at p. 190.

2. *Thinking How to Live*, pp. 268–69.

3. In using the term "incomparable" rather than the more common "incommensurable," I follow Gibbard in his "Reply to Critics," in the symposium on *Thinking How to Live* in *Philosophy and Phenomenological Research*.

4. Preference here is strict preference: to prefer x over y involves *not* preferring y over x.

5. T. M. Scanlon independently raises this issue in his "Reasons and Decisions." Gibbard replies to Scanlon in his "Reply to Critics." Both essays are in the symposium on *Thinking How to Live* in *Philosophy and Phenomenological Research*.

6. This question takes us into the territory of recent work on the relation between reasons and what John Broome calls normative requirements. See, for example, Broome, "Does Rationality Give Us Reasons?" (2005).

7. In his first book, for example, Gibbard remarks that "the key to human moral nature . . . lies in *coordination* broadly conceived." And it is clear that he is here referring to social coordination. See *Wise Choices, Apt Feelings* (1990) at p. 26.

8. I emphasize the coordinating roles of planning in my *Intention, Plans, and Practical Reason* (1987; 1999). I return to these matters, and to associated debates with J. David Velleman, in my "Intention, Belief, Practical, Theoretical" (forthcoming).

9. We can also wonder, when we return to the level of normative thinking about reasons, whether we do indeed have reason to agglomerate all such wild contingency plans.

10. Indeed, this appeal to plans for weighing is in the spirit of Gibbard's earlier, 1990 theory according to which, roughly, "to say that an act is rational . . . is to express one's acceptance of a system of norms for weighing considerations that, as things come out, supports doing that." *Wise Choices, Apt Feelings* (1990), p. 163. I discuss these matters further in my "*Thinking How to Live* and the Restriction Problem," where I consider a "higher-order Sartre case" that I put to one side here. Gibbard's reply is in his "Reply to Critics."

11. And see *Thinking How to Live*, pp. 271–74.

12. This theme is developed in *Thinking How to Live*, chap. 14, where Gibbard distinguishes between different versions of such shared thinking.

13. In a generalization of this case, you are what Gibbard calls a judgment individualist. See *Thinking How to Live*, pp. 272–74. I discuss this kind of individualist in my "*Thinking How to Live* and the Restriction Problem," and Gibbard responds in his "Reply to Critics."

Comments on Allan Gibbard's
Tanner Lectures

John Broome

It was a great privilege to be invited to Allan Gibbard's lectures, and to comment on them. Gibbard has made extraordinary contributions to widely separated areas of ethics. He is a leading figure in the expressivist approach to metaethics, and he has also made huge advances in first-order ethical theory, often by bringing to bear the formal methods of decision theory and game theory. His Tanner Lectures integrate these apparently very different subjects. They show us how his first-order theory is motivated by his metaethics—specifically by his view that ethical questions are planning questions.

I admire this integration, but I am sorry to say I have not been able to imitate it. I have decided to take up two separate issues, one from Lecture I and one from Lecture III.

Comment on Lecture I

Take an ought sentence such as 'Brutus ought not to have conspired against Caesar' or 'I ought to be careful here.' Philosophers used to worry about whether sentences like this could be true or false, and many denied they could be. But these days we worry less about that. Most philosophers nowadays think it is not so hard for sentences of a particular class to meet the criteria that allow them to count as true or false. They need only to participate in our thinking and talking in characteristic ways. For example, we need to treat them as subject to truth-functional logic. We need to be able to make sense of disagreement about them, when some of us assert a sentence and others deny it. We need to recognize that a sentence might be true even though no one is in a position to assert it justifiably. And so on. Since ought sentences meet these standards, they can be true or false. Consequently, we can have cognitive attitudes toward these sentences or toward their contents. We can believe or disbelieve them, or what they say.

That is no longer very controversial. We can accept that ought sentences are true or false because of what we do with them. But this leaves us with the task of explaining why we do those things with them. How come these sentences participate in our thinking and talking in ways that are characteristic of truth?

If we were dealing with sentences about natural things, the answer to this question would emerge from the relation between these sentences and the facts of the world. Sentences about natural things are true or false in virtue of their relation to the world. That explains why our thinking and talking treats them in the ways that are characteristic of truth. We could give a parallel answer for ought sentences: We could say they are true or false in virtue of their relation to the normative facts of the world. But Gibbard and many other philosophers find that answer fantastic. It seems incredible to them that the world contains such normative facts. So they look for an alternative explanation.

Gibbard offers one. He offers an explanation of why we use ought sentences, and why we use them in such a way that they earn the right to count as true or false. His detailed explanation appears in his book *Thinking How to Live* (Harvard, 2003). His Lecture I contains an outline of his explanation.

It is that these sentences help us to plan our lives in general, and to plan what to do on particular occasions. He says that, when we utter an ought sentence, we are (to a first approximation) expressing a partial plan. It is a natural fact about us that we make plans.

Consequently, as Gibbard emphasizes, his explanation of the truth of ought sentences does not assume that anything exists apart from the natural world. It does not assume there are normative facts in the world.

Gibbard explains in detail how, as our thinking and talking use these sentences to express our plans and develop our planning, they endow the sentences with the characteristics of truth and falsity. For one thing, in *Thinking How to Live* he provides a semantic theory that explains how they participate in truth-functional logic. The details do not matter here.

Since ought sentences have the characteristics of truth and falsity, that explains how we have the attitudes of belief and disbelief toward them. These cognitive attitudes are explained on the basis of the noncognitive attitudes that are involved in planning. Indeed, they simply *are* those noncognitive attitudes in another guise. To believe you ought not to feel resentment is just to plan not to feel resentment. To believe Brutus ought not to have conspired against Caesar is just to plan not to conspire against Caesar in the counterfactual situation of being Brutus as the Ides of March approach.

Gibbard argues that planning attitudes, if they are rational, are connected together in a structure that mimics the structure of rational believing attitudes. This explains why the sentences that express the planning attitudes have the logical structure of truth. It allows us to treat our planning attitudes as ought beliefs. These attitudes are fundamentally noncognitive, but they earn the right to count as cognitive. Each is a planning attitude and also a believing attitude. That is to say, each attitude has the property of being a noncognitive planning attitude, and also the property of being a cognitive believing attitude. But the property of being a noncognitive attitude is the fundamental one, in that it explains the property of being a cognitive attitude.

So ought beliefs are plans, to a first approximation. There are two reasons that this is only an approximation. One of them is mentioned by Gibbard himself. Not all plans are ought beliefs. When you are indifferent between two options, you will not believe you ought to take one of them, nor that you ought to take the other. But unless you are as foolish as Buridan's ass, you will plan to take one or else plan to take the other. So you may plan to do something without believing you ought to do it.

Because of this, Gibbard's theory is not exactly as I have described it so far. Gibbard does not say that ought beliefs are exactly attitudes of planning. Instead, he says they are founded on what he calls a 'valenced' attitude. This attitude might be called 'okaying.' (This is my name; Gibbard does not use 'okay' as a verb.) Okaying is a noncognitive attitude. It is like the attitude of planning, but weaker. Buridan's ass okayed eating the left bale and also okayed eating the right bale, but it did not plan to eat the left bale and also plan to eat the right one. Indeed, it did not plan to eat either. A more sensible creature would have planned to eat one or the other, but it would not have planned to eat one and also planned to eat the other.

The noncognitive attitude of okaying corresponds to the cognitive attitude of believing okay. I hesitate to attribute to an ass cognitive attitudes that have a normative content, because it may not be clever enough to possess them. But an adult human being can possess them. So when an adult human being okays an action, she believes it is okay. We can now also specify the cognitive attitude of believing one ought to do something. To believe one ought to do something is to okay doing it and decline to okay not doing it. Once again, it is the noncognitive attitudes of okaying and declining to okay that are fundamental. But because they participate in our thinking and talking in ways that are characteristic of truth, they earn the right to count as cognitive attitudes too.

That is one reason that Gibbard's initial formulation is just an approximation. The second is one he does not mention. The attitude of believing you ought to do something simply is not the attitude of planning to do it. Gibbard says that thinking what you ought to do is thinking what to do. But it is not. Thinking what you ought to do is to ask yourself, "What ought I to do?" whereas to think what to do is to ask, "What shall I do?" These are different questions, and they may have different answers.

"What shall I do?" is not a typical sort of question. To answer a typical question, you simply express a belief. If you ask yourself, "Where are my keys?" and answer, "Beside the phone," your answer simply expresses your belief that your keys are beside the phone. But if you ask, "What shall I do?" and answer, "Read the newspaper," your answer expresses more than a belief. It expresses an intention to read the newspaper. Gibbard would call your question a 'planning question.' In asking it, you call on yourself to form an intention. True, by the time you come to answer, "Read the newspaper," you believe you will read the newspaper. That is because, in forming your intention to read the newspaper, you acquire the belief that you will do so. Your answer expresses your belief as well as your intention. But the special feature of your question is that it calls on you to form an intention.

"What ought I to do?" is a typical question, at least on the face of it. It calls for an answer that expresses a belief. If you answer it, "Start writing that lecture," you express the belief that you ought to start writing that lecture. However, Gibbard treats this too as a planning question. Maybe it is, but it is certainly not the same as the simple planning question, "What shall I do?" If its answer constitutes a plan, it does not constitute a plan of the simplest sort, such as your plan to read the newspaper. At the same time as you answer the question "What ought I to do?" with "Start writing that lecture," you might answer the question "What shall I do?" with "Read the newspaper." Then you would plan to read the newspaper while believing you ought to start writing that lecture.

If you give these answers, what you plan to do is something other than what you believe you ought to do. This means you are akratic. We have to recognize that akrasia is possible. It follows that thinking what you ought to do is not thinking what to do.

This does not mean Gibbard is wrong to treat our ought beliefs as fundamentally noncognitive attitudes. They may be, but they are further from ordinary planning attitudes than he suggests. Gibbard only says they are "like" planning attitudes. That remains possible. They could resemble planning attitudes, even though they are rather far removed from our ordinary planning attitudes. They could be some sort of *ideal* planning attitudes—not what we actually mundanely plan but what we plan ideally in some way or other.

Suppose these attitudes are some sort of ideal plans. Gibbard recognizes anyway that they must be idealized, because of another feature of them. We have beliefs about what all sorts of people ought to do in all sorts of circumstances. If these are to be construed as plans, they must be plans that are conditional on remote and impossible conditions. For instance, if you believe Brutus ought not to have conspired against Caesar, you must have a plan that is conditional on your being Brutus. As a planning attitude, this is very idealized.

I think the remoteness of these ideal attitudes from ordinary planning raises a serious problem for Gibbard. These attitudes are the foundation of his account of normativity. They are fundamentally noncognitive, though they can earn the right to count as beliefs. But how can we identify these attitudes and know what attitudes they are?

We can generally identify people's ordinary plans rather easily. If you plan to read the newspaper, your plan is a disposition of yours that will, among other things, typically cause you to read the newspaper. That makes it easy to recognize. The disposition that constitutes a plan is complex, but its details can be spelled out; many of them are spelled out in Michael Bratman's *Intention, Plans and Practical Reason* (Harvard, 1987). In any case, we are very familiar with ordinary plans as part of the regular commerce of our lives. Often, we easily recognize our own plans and other people's, through our ordinary understanding of our psychology and theirs.

But frequently, the ideal attitudes Gibbard calls on can be identified only through the properties they have as cognitive attitudes. Take the attitude of okaying something. This is the noncognitive attitude that founds, explains, and constitutes the cognitive attitude of believing the thing is okay. Are you familiar with this attitude of okaying? I think you will be able to recognize it only as the cognitive attitude of believing the thing is okay. I do not think you have any other way to grasp what this attitude is.

Or take the attitude of planning ideally to start writing that lecture, while at the same time you plan mundanely to read the newspaper. No doubt you are familiar with the mundane plan and can identify it easily. It is a disposition that will probably cause you to read the newspaper. On the way, it may cause you to get out of your chair, go to collect the newspaper from the table, and so on. But are you familiar with the ideal planning attitude that, in this case, is to start writing that lecture? Once again, I think you will only be able to identify it as your cognitive attitude of believing you ought to start writing that lecture. Likewise with your attitude of planning not to conspire against Caesar, if you are Brutus—I suspect you will recognize that attitude only by recognizing it as your belief that Brutus ought not to have conspired against Caesar.

This is how I think you are going to have to identify the ideal planning attitudes that Gibbard is talking about. You will have to recognize them as normative beliefs. This method will not steer you wrong. So far as Gibbard is concerned, you will identify the right attitudes this way, since ideal planning attitudes (provided you do indeed have them) are indeed normative beliefs. They have both the property of being planning attitudes and the property of being normative beliefs. So I am not contradicting what Gibbard is saying.

However, I do think this point about identification puts in doubt Gibbard's project of explaining our normative beliefs. The underlying noncognitive attitudes are supposed to explain how we have the cognitive attitudes. More accurately, an attitude's property of being a planning attitude is supposed to explain how it has the property of being a normative belief. But we can only recognize the underlying noncognitive attitude by recognizing its property of being a cognitive attitude. Gibbard in effect tells us that the belief that you ought to start writing that lecture is explained by the noncognitive attitude, whatever it is, that you recognize as the belief that you ought to start writing that lecture.

The explanans is identified through the explanandum, and this happens extensively throughout the explanatory story. This makes me doubt that we are being given much of an explanation at all. For a proper explanation, we should have some independent means of recognizing the explanans.

More particularly, my doubt is this. Gibbard's idea is that the noncognitive, planning attitudes, provided they are rational, are supposed to be woven together in a structure that explains how they can be treated as beliefs. But now it emerges that these attitudes can be identified in the first place only through their derived property of being beliefs. This means that, if they are rational, they cannot help having the structure of rational beliefs anyway. Attitudes that are identified by their cognitive aspect cannot, if they are rational, help standing in the relations that rational cognitive attitudes stand in. The explanation of why they stand in these relations is that they are rational cognitive attitudes. Gibbard's story is that they stand in these relations because they are rational planning attitudes, but actually it is because they are rational beliefs. It is not that planning attitudes earn the right to count as cognitive attitudes; they have this right because we identify them as cognitive attitudes.

Comment on Lecture III

Gibbard gives great credit to Harsanyi in developing his utilitarian version of contractualism. He reminds us that Harsanyi in the 1950s proved two distinct theorems that can be used to support utilitarianism. The first makes use of the ideas that Rawls later called 'the original position' and 'the veil of ignorance.' So that theorem is directly in the contractualist tradition, but the second is not. Nevertheless, Gibbard recruits the second theorem as well as the first to support his contractualist position.

One special feature of Gibbard's contractualism is that he thinks morality requires us to settle on a common goal, which each of us should pursue. He objects (p. 64) to a moral theory that allows each person to pursue her own distinct goals. He points out that, if we do each pursue our own goals, we shall encounter prisoners' dilemmas. The effect will be that everyone ends up satisfying her goals less well than they would have been satisfied had we all cooperated in pursuing common goals. Gibbard says (pp. 66–67):

> Whatever reasons each has for the peculiarities of her own goals, there is a way better to advance, in prospect, all these goals at once. The way is to agree on a common scale of goals for all to pursue.

Gibbard uses Harsanyi's second theorem to support this claim. He also uses it to support a second, subsidiary claim that this common goal is utilitarian in a broad sense: It is a weighted average of the goals of individuals (p. 67).

To be more accurate, Gibbard supports these claims, not with Harsanyi's own theorem, but with what he calls a 'Harsanyi-like' theorem. His appendix describes this theorem and illustrates it in a diagram. My figure B1 is a copy of this diagram. The axes show values of the variables v_i and v_j, which are two people's 'goal-scales'; they measure the degrees to which the people's goals are satisfied. Each point in the diagram marks a combination of values for v_i and v_j. The curve is the frontier of the set of points that are feasible; points on or below this frontier are feasible; points above it are not. We assume that one of the feasible points is ideal. We assume a 'Paretian' condition for this ideal. That is to say, we assume an arrangement is not ideal if it is possible to better satisfy one of the people's goals without satisfying the other person's goals less well.

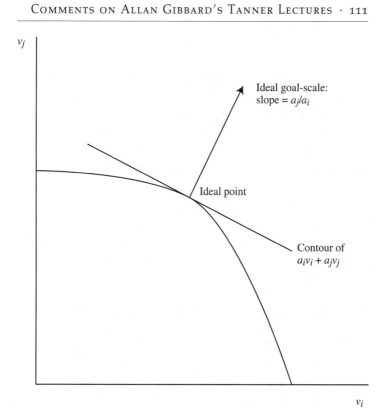

Figure B1

This ensures that the ideal point is on the frontier. We also assume that the set of feasible points is strictly convex, which means that the frontier bows outward.

Given these assumptions, the theorem Gibbard appeals to says that there is some weighted average $(a_i v_i + a_j v_j)$ of v_i and v_j such that the ideal point maximizes this average among the points in the feasible set and is the only point to do so. The tangent in figure B1 is a contour of this weighted average. A line perpendicular to the contour has slope a_j/a_i. Gibbard calls the weighted average the "ideal goal-scale." The theorem generalizes from two to many people, but this two-person example is enough for what I need to say.

I do not think Gibbard should call this theorem 'Harsanyi-like'; I see little resemblance between it and Harsanyi's second theorem. It is one of the elementary theorems of convex analysis. I shall call it 'the tangent theorem.' As Gibbard points out, geometrically the theorem simply says that, at any point on the frontier of a strictly convex set, a tangent can be drawn that meets the set at that point only.

Moreover, I do not think the tangent theorem offers any worthwhile support to Gibbard's view that we should pursue common goals. It tells us that the ideal point could be achieved by maximizing the ideal goal-scale Gibbard defines. But it is a big step from there to the conclusion that we should pursue common goals. Gibbard himself mentions one difficulty in making that step. Even if we all independently pursue common goals, we may together fail to achieve those goals, because we may fail to coordinate our individual actions properly. But, as he explains (p. 85), Gibbard himself long ago proved a theorem that overcomes this difficulty in some circumstances. It is not this difficulty that concerns me.

The difficulty that concerns me is that, for all the tangent theorem tells us, the ideal goal-scale may depend on the shape of the feasible set, and on where in the feasible set the ideal point is. Alterations in the feasible set will change the ideal point, and we have no reason to think they will not alter the ideal goal-scale. We therefore cannot know what the ideal goal-scale is until we know what the feasible set is and which point in it is the ideal one. But in view of the complexity of life, we cannot possibly know the shape of the feasible set, and we certainly cannot know the position of the ideal point.

Figure B2 illustrates. It shows the frontiers of two possible feasible sets. I have picked out ideal points on each of these frontiers. Our theorem tells us nothing about where they are, so I have picked them arbitrarily.

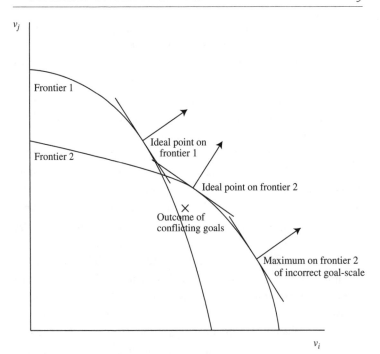

Figure B2

The two I have picked would be achieved by maximizing different ideal goal-scales within their respective feasible sets. We have no way of knowing which is the right goal-scale to maximize. We might easily get it wrong, averaging the two people's individual scales using the wrong weights. Then, if we maximized our wrong scale, we might end up far from the ideal point. Indeed, we might end up in a worse position than we would have reached if the two people had separately pursued their own goals. To be sure, we would end up somewhere on the frontier rather than inside it, as figure B2 shows. And to be sure too, if the people pursued their own disparate goals, they might end up somewhere inside the frontier, because of bother with prisoners' dilemmas. Nevertheless, the point they end up at might be better than the one achieved by maximizing the wrong goal-scale. Inevitably, some points inside the frontier are better than some points that are on the frontier.

We therefore cannot conclude that we necessarily advance our goals better by choosing common goals to pursue.

For a different reason, the tangent theorem also does not support the subsidiary claim that, if we do choose a common goal-scale, it should be a weighted average of individual goal-scales. True, it tells us that the ideal point can be achieved by maximizing a weighted average of individual goal-scales. But there are many other functions such that the ideal point can be reached by maximizing one of them. For example, figure B3 shows it can be reached by maximizing a minimum function, specifically the function $\min\{(v_i - v^*_i), (v_j - v^*_j)\}$, where v^*_i and v^*_j are the values of the individuals' goal-scales achieved at the ideal point. Indeed, maximizing this sort of minimum function has an advantage over maximizing a weighted average. Figure 3 shows it will work even when the feasible set is not convex.

All in all, the tangent theorem is far too weak to give worthwhile support to any sort of utilitarianism. It will not do what Gibbard asks it to do. But Harsanyi's second theorem is very much more powerful; indeed, its conclusion is remarkable. Here is a statement of it. To match Gibbard's purposes, I have interpreted it in terms of goals and goal-scales.

Assume:

1. Each person's goals are coherent (which means they satisfy the axioms of expected utility theory).
2. The common goals are coherent.
3. The common goals satisfy the 'Paretian' condition: that if each person's goals are indifferent between two prospects, then the common goals are indifferent between those prospects; and if one person's goals place the first of two prospects above the second, and no person's goals place the second above the first, then the common goals place the first above the second.

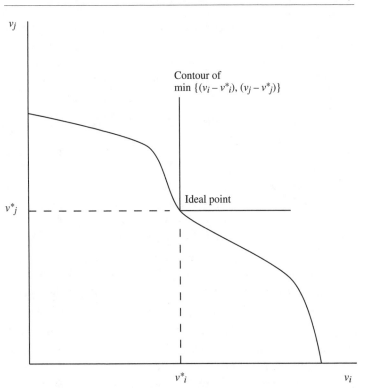

Figure B3

Then:

The common goals can be represented by an expectational goal-scale that is a weighted average of expectational goal-scales that represent the goals of the individuals.

(A goal-scale is said to *represent* a set of goals if and only if, whenever the goals rank one prospect at least as high as a second, the first has at least as high a value on the goal-scale as the second. A goal-scale is said to be *expectational* if and only if the value it assigns to a prospect is the expectation of the values it assigns to the prospect's possible outcomes.)

This theorem is illustrated in figure B4. It tells us that all points in the diagram can be ranked by the common goals in a way that is independent of the feasible set and of the ideal point. It therefore gives the people something they can agree on without knowing the feasible set or the ideal point. Whatever the feasible set turns out to be, the ideal point will always be whatever point in that set maximizes the common goal-scale. Moreover, the theorem tells us that these common goals are a weighted average of the individuals' goals.

This is just what Gibbard needs. So in the end, I think he is right to say that Harsanyi's second theorem gives him what he needs, but wrong to suggest that a weaker surrogate will do.

Moreover, this theorem would give him more than he seems to realize. He says (p. 70), "I find it hard to see how a coherent goal-scale can have any rationale other than that it sums up the weight of a set of considerations. I don't know how to establish definitively that it must . . . ." Well, Harsanyi's theorem establishes it. That is why this theorem is remarkable. One of its premises is that each person's goals are a consideration; each person's goals count. That is what the Paretian condition says, in effect. Simply on the basis of the coherence conditions and this assumption that each person's goals count, the theorem concludes that they count specifically in an additive fashion. Their weights are added. The theorem derives additivity from those remarkably weak premises. Gibbard does not need to assume additivity; he could take it from the theorem.

Furthermore, the theorem answers a question Gibbard raises at the end of the appendix. He says (p. 87), "I have considered only a fixed feasible set of prospects. We can ask, then, whether the social contracts that are ideal for different possible circumstances . . . all maximize the same goal-scale." The answer from Harsanyi's theorem is: "Yes, they do." As I explained, the goal-scale is independent of the feasible set of prospects.

Given all the merits of Harsanyi's own theorem, why did Gibbard eschew it and instead fall back on a theorem that turns out too

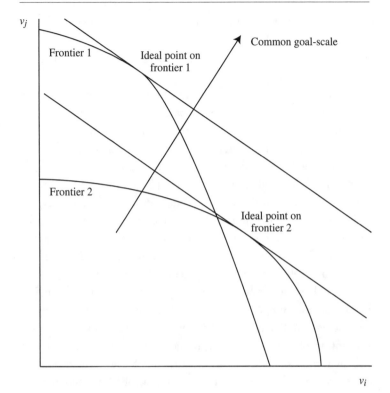

Figure B4

weak for his purposes? His answer is explicit on p. 65. It is that he thinks the second premise of Harsanyi's theorem—that the common goals are coherent—is open to question. But I have explained that he needs this premise. He cannot happily give it up and fall back on a weaker theorem, because the weaker theorem is not up to the work he demands from it. I therefore think he needs to try to establish the coherence of the common goals. If the common goals are indeed not coherent, that will do serious damage to the argument of his Lecture III. It will weaken his case for a utilitarian type of contractualism.

I agree with Gibbard that the coherence of the common goals is open to question. Nevertheless, the answer to this question might be that they are. I do not know. I do have my own arguments in defence of the second premise of Harsanyi's theorem; they are set out in my book *Weighing Goods* (Blackwell, 1991). But I interpret the theorem differently from Gibbard—in terms of good rather than goals. I take it to be telling us something about the structure of good, and specifically about how the overall good is related to the good of individuals. Under this interpretation, I believe Harsanyi's theorem can be used to give strong support to utilitarianism, or more exactly to a utilitarian theory of value. Under my interpretation, the theorem's first premise is that the good of each individual is coherent, and the second premise is that overall good is coherent. I believe these premises can be convincingly defended. In particular, I believe that overall good is coherent.

But Gibbard does not wish to interpret the theorem in terms of good. For one thing, doing so would not be so conducive to his contractualism. Furthermore, in view of T. M. Scanlon's attack on the notion of individual good, he does not wish to rely on this notion at this point in his argument (p. 66). So he turns instead to the more general notion of an individual's goals. Correspondingly, he turns to common goals instead of overall good.

However, he does actually accept a notion of overall good, and he takes it for granted that the common goals achieve overall good. "By the overall good," he says (p. 67), "I shall mean good as measured by whatever goal-scale would be specified by the social contract." If we may take this assumption seriously, then my own arguments for coherence will apply to the common goals, because they apply to overall good. So I see some prospect of justifying the second premise of Harsanyi's theorem, even under Gibbard's interpretation. I cannot say more than that, because much more work would be needed to develop a full defence. It would have to be explained how we can be sure that the common goals do indeed achieve something that can count as overall good.

My point is that Gibbard cannot satisfactorily evade this work. Though he does not realize it, for his purposes, he needs the common goal-scale to be coherent. He needs to use the genuine version of Harsanyi's second theorem; a weaker substitute is not enough.

Should You Save This Child? Gibbard on Intuitions, Contractualism, and Strains of Commitment

F. M. KAMM

Of the many topics dealt with in Allan Gibbard's rich and challenging Tanner Lectures, I shall focus on three: (1) the nature and significance of intuitions; (2) disagreements about the correct form of contractualist reasoning; and (3) whether each person's acting for a shared goal is at once most rational and yet something that we can reasonably reject. I shall begin with some thoughts on the first topic, for I suspect that I have the honor of commenting on these lectures because I rely so heavily in my own work on intuitive judgments about cases.

1. Gibbard begins his first lecture by discussing the views of psychologist Jonathan Haidt, who claims that we do not reason our way to moral conclusions but rather respond intuitively and then find reasons to support "preordained conclusions." Mostly, according to Haidt, reasoning constructs "justifications of intuitive judgments, causing the illusion of objective reasoning."[1] Gibbard compares this to lawyers who have to find reasons to support the side whose advocates they are.

One of my concerns with Haidt's view is his claim that finding justifications of intuitive judgments, after having the judgments, can only create an illusion of objectivity. Suppose someone has an intuitive response and then tries to find out what it is about the act or situation she is considering that accounts for her response. In having the intuitive judgment, unlike a lawyer, she does not merely pick (or get assigned to defend) a position; she is drawn to it as correct. Once she locates the factors that account for her response, she can consider whether these factors not only account for her response but, on reflection, justify it. If they do, then this might be evidence that the intuition was the result of very rapidly and unconsciously "reasoning" from these factors to a judgment. In any case, if the intuitive judgment is justified on reflection, it is an instance of a correct judgment and, in this sense, objectively correct. The intuitive judgment is no less objectively true if awareness of the factors and reasoning that justify it comes after the judgment than if such awareness comes before, contrary to what Haidt suggests. Of course, the grounds for the intuition may not justify the judgment, in which case one might need an error theory in order to account for the illusion of correctness. Furthermore, one would seek to avoid relying on the intuition, if it remains even after its inadequate grounds are uncovered.

In this process of seeing whether there are justifications for intuitive judgments, we may move back to other intuitive judgments. For example, if we intuitively judge that we may turn a trolley away from five people and in a direction where it will hit one person, part of the ground we can subsequently uncover for this intuition may be the intuitive judgments that one person being killed is better than five people being killed and that death is bad for people. These intuitive judgments may (or may not) have deeper grounds that can be uncovered. Gibbard thinks that intuitions are basic judgments, ones not based on other judgments: "An intuition ... is a state of mind of accepting something, not on the basis of further reasoning even upon challenge."[2] My sense (as exemplified by the trolley case just described) is that the term should not be limited to only the most basic judgments for which we could uncover no further grounds. Gibbard and I can agree, however, that what I would call nonbasic intuitions can be had without being aware of further justifying grounds for them that could be uncovered, and that there are some very basic intuitions that lack further grounds to be uncovered.

Gibbard's concern is why we should place any stock in intuitions if we accept a naturalistic picture of the world. In such a world picture, moral intuitions cannot give us insight into nonnatural facts that could support the truth of these judgments. In Gibbard's view, a naturalistic picture of the world reveals that people, in order to survive and reproduce successfully, must not only have accurate beliefs about the way the world is empirically, but must also plan what to do and feel. There are no answers to these planning questions, he says, given by the natural world. However, planning what to do will involve weighing considerations such as pleasure and pain, and "weighing enjoyment in favor and suffering against, on no further ground, amounts to having an intuition about why to do things. Intuitions, then, apply to planning, and not just to thinking how things stand. If I keep challenging my thoughts about what to do and why, I end up grounding my planning in intuition."[3] But again, he notes, the question arises: "Why think we can intuit why to do things? . . . Why think we can intuit why and why not to feel certain ways about things?"[4]

According to Gibbard, "thinking of ought judgments as plans leads to an answer. . . . To say that I have this intuition is just another way of saying that I confidently weigh the chance of suffering against doing a thing, and on no further grounds even if I ask myself why."[5] So far this answer to "Why think we can intuit what to do and feel?" just seems to amount to the claim that we are capable of confidently weighing some factor, and on no further grounds, even if we ask ourselves why. This is only an empirical, de facto sense of intuition, Gibbard says. In a normative, de jure sense, "an intuition . . . is a state of mind of accepting something, not on the basis of further reasoning even upon challenge, that we *ought* to place some trust in." And if we accept his account of ought judgments, according to which they are like plans to do or prefer to do something, this can yield his claim that "[t]o think something an intuition in this sense is to *plan* to rely on it.... It's a normative claim, then, that de facto intuitions are genuine intuitions—and one we need ... for coherent planning."[6]

Any plan to rely on a nonderived judgment is subject to evaluation; we should not ultimately adopt the plan to rely on our nonderived judgment if it fails the test for being a good plan. Gibbard thinks that the test for good planning to rely on an intuition is whether we would plan to rely on it in a situation that is ideal for making plans. This is a situation in which "what I would then *think* ought to be done *ought* to be done."[7] Some of the characteristics of such an ideal situation might be, he says, "full information vividly taken in and contemplated, and an alert, engaged, and dispassionate frame of mind."[8] But he does not think that there is yet a complete and unproblematic characterization of the conditions under which to trust one's normative judgments.

Here are some questions I have about Gibbard's answer to why we should place stock in our intuitions given a naturalistic worldview. In one sense, Gibbard's answer to why we should think that we can have genuine intuitions seems to imply that it is *necessary* that we have genuine intuitions. For, on his account, we are (naturalistically speaking) planning creatures, and we could not plan if we did not have intuitions that we thought we ought to rely on, intuitions that we thought were genuine. But, of course, these are only intuitions that we think are genuine; we could actually be planning with intuitions on which we ought not to rely (e.g., on which we would not plan to rely in an ideal planning situation). Many who think we can, in fact, have genuine intuitions are willing to accept that we might not have been able to have them, even while remaining planning creatures. Indeed, they are open to the idea that we may not, in fact, have them and we could be mistaken in thinking that we have them. The cognitive, as opposed to planning, approach to intuitions is certainly not committed to its being necessary that we have genuine intuitions. On the planning approach as well, it seems that we could not be sure that we had genuine intuitions unless we would form plans to rely on empirical intuitions in an ideal planning situation. Hence, the planning approach will not explain the genuineness of any intuitions unless, at least, we know both what the characteristics of an ideal planning situation are and that we can be sure that we actually ever occupy it.

But suppose there were no sense in which intuitions are genuine other than that we would decide, when we are in a state of full information, alert, dispassionate, etc., to plan to rely on them. What reason is there to think that one plan about what to do and feel in the realm of morality would be any better than another plan, or that it would pay to plan at all, unless being in such a state allowed us to be aware of reasons for doing and feeling that are present independently of what we plan to rely on in that state?

I conclude that the reasons for which Gibbard accepts "that normative thinking rests on intuition"[9] are not intended to, and do not, give comfort to the many who ordinarily place stock in intuition, even those consequentialists who employ only very basic intuitions such as that pleasure is good and pain is bad. However, he does help to undermine the position of those who claim to be able to do ethics without intuitions in any sense.

2. Gibbard begins his second lecture by contrasting two approaches to morality. The first is what he calls humanistic. It approaches morality as something that has value because it is of value to humanity in a way "that can be appreciated in nonethical terms." I take this to mean that it approaches morality as a way of achieving nonmoral goods for humanity. This approach, he says, may be based on the intuition that humanity matters (and so it matters that they have nonmoral goods). The second approach is "intuitionistic, in one important sense of that term," he says. It relies very heavily on intuitions, seeks to systematize them, and hopes to "uncover a deep, implicit rationale for our intuitive responses" that "will turn

out to be a worthy one." This hope, he thinks, implies that "the two broad styles converge."[10]

Gibbard's description of what he calls the humanistic approach suggests that it takes an instrumental approach to morality: Morality is a means to achieving nonmoral goods. Gibbard's favoring the humanistic approach may, therefore, be in some tension with his subsequent embrace of the framework of Scanlonian contractualism, for Scanlon's view is that the point of morality is to act in ways that we can justify to others, and that we can do this (roughly) if we act on principles that no one (who was seeking principles for living with others) could reasonably reject. Being able to live on these terms with others will require us to consider the nonmoral good of others because this good helps determine what they could and could not reasonably reject. But the goal of getting agreement and justifying one's conduct to others is not a mere means to securing nonmoral goods. Scanlon says, "It is, in a more fundamental sense, what morality is about."[11] If this is what morality is about, it seems to me that its value cannot be appreciated in nonethical terms.

Gibbard's description of the intuitionist approach coincides with the one I gave at the beginning of my comments on Lecture I, except for his inference that "worthy" rationales for intuitions are ones that show morality to be for humanity in the sense of providing benefits that can be appreciated in nonethical terms.

Consider in more detail what Gibbard thinks it is for morality to be for humanity. He thinks it consists in satisfying humanistic preferences, which are preferences for the benefit of all humanity. The minimal sense of this is that if one prospect will be better than a second for everyone, then it is ethically better.[12] (This is the prospective Pareto condition put in terms of the good of people; it does not necessarily coincide with the satisfaction of preferences they have for their own sake, for these might be mistaken.) A more robust interpretation is that morality seeks the maximal good for people, understood as the maximal sum of individual utilities, and thus the maximal expected utility for each individual behind a veil of ignorance.

I think there are reasons to doubt, first, that morality is only for persons (or sentient beings) and, second, that the parts of it that are for persons take the form of arrangements that produce maximal expected utility for individuals from behind a veil of ignorance.

A. Consider the first point. Thomas Scanlon claims that there is a part of morality that is concerned with impersonal values, though he believes it is not the part that contractualism explains. For example, it would be morally wrong to pave over the Grand Canyon or to destroy great works of art, even if this were not bad for people.[13] This is a part of morality that is not about people. Shelly Kagan and Larry Temkin[14] argue that there is a part of morality that is about people but not about doing as much good for them as possible. They argue that the Pareto condition (even in terms of good rather than preferences) is wrong: It can be morally worse if someone gets what is good for him even if his getting it is not worse for anyone else. Consider an evil person who has utility 20 and a good person who has utility 10. It could simply be morally better if people have only as much good as they deserve in absolute terms, and also better if their relative utility is in proportion to their desert. If this is so, it could be morally better if the evil person had less utility, thereby giving him what he deserves in absolute terms, even if this did not improve anyone else's condition. It would also be better if the evil person's utility were less than the good person's, at least if this is not below the point of his absolute desert, even though this does not improve the condition of the good person (or anyone else).

B. Now consider some questions about Gibbard's view that to the extent to which morality is for people (in the sense of for people's good), it involves giving each individual his highest prospective utility from behind a veil of ignorance, and that this is the system no one could reasonably reject once it is ongoing, as each would have agreed to it behind a veil of ignorance when deciding for his own good.

Gibbard begins by arguing that while nothing in his metaethics commits one to planning to live with others on terms of mutual respect, this seems like an intuitively plausible plan. (He does not say that anything about persons *demands* that one plan to live in this way with them.) Such mutual respect, he agrees with Scanlon, involves treating each person in ways he could not reasonably reject. This further involves, he thinks, treating people in accord with principles or arrangements they would have agreed to from an impartial point of view, that is, without their knowing what position they would actually occupy. In Lecture II, Gibbard follows Harsanyi and Rawls, not Scanlon, in thinking that this involves treating each as he would have agreed to be treated from behind a veil of ignorance, when each chooses for his own good.[15] He follows Harsanyi, but not Rawls, in thinking that choosing from behind a veil of ignorance involves choosing under an assumption that one has an equal probability of being any person in any actual position in society. He follows Harsanyi in thinking that a correct choice from behind the veil of ignorance would be for a system that maximizes each person's prospective average utility, on the assumption that each person would adhere to what such a system requires. (Strains of commitment that would jeopardize adherence eventually have to be considered in deciding what principles to select.) If it will maximize each person's prospective average utility to risk being very poor when others are very rich, then a person who actually turns out to be poor is being treated respectfully when called upon to remain poor, as he would have chosen such a system when deciding for his own good from behind the veil of ignorance.

In Gibbard's view,[16] the challenge for a contractualist is to derive something other than this utilitarian principle, for, he thinks, a nonutilitarian principle is one that no one would choose behind a veil of ignorance when choosing for his own good (assuming adherence by all); he would only choose such a nonutilitarian principle if he knew what position he would actually occupy.

(i) My first concern is whether Gibbard's intuitive endorsement of a ground-level plan to live on terms of mutual respect with others coheres with his other views. Suppose we have not yet derived his further view that treating someone with respect specifically amounts to treating him in accord with principles he would have agreed to for his own prospective good behind a veil of ignorance. Then, it remains open that taking the risk of falling into a position in which one is treated *disrespectfully* will prospectively maximize one's chances of achieving nonethical goods. Hence, given Gibbard's view that a humanistic perspective on morality makes essential reference to achieving nonethical goods for humanity, it is not clear why he accepts (prior to deciding what respect specifically implies) that planning how to live with others should, at its base, involve planning to live on terms of mutual respect with each person. It seems that at its base, his plan of how to live with others should involve a commitment to maximizing nonethical goods for humanity.[17]

Of course, Gibbard does give a particular interpretation of respectful treatment in Lecture II that involves being treated in accordance with principles to which one would have agreed on one's own behalf behind a veil of ignorance. This implies that, by definition, one *could* not, behind the veil of ignorance, agree to risk being in a *disrespectful* position as a means of maximizing one's prospective average utility. Even being treated as a mere thing could not, on Gibbard's view, be termed an intrinsically disrespectful position if agreeing to risk being so treated were a concomitant of choosing what would maximize one's prospective average utility. I find this an implausible implication of his view (and will comment on it further below).[18]

(ii) Gibbard is attempting to find a place for Harsanyi's utilitarian conclusion within a Scanlonian framework. So let us next consider the contrast between Scanlon and Harsanyi on contractualism.

Gibbard believes that he can locate a disagreement between Scanlon and Harsanyi in the problem of identifying a conception of a person's good that can play a role in moral theory, and in particular in the choice behind the veil. While it may be true that Harsanyi and Scanlon differ in the way Gibbard thinks they do, I do not think that Scanlon's objections to Harsanyi would be limited to the problem of identifying a morally relevant conception of a person's good. In his early article "Contractualism and Utilitarianism,"[19] Scanlon directly argues against Harsanyi and the sort of reasoning behind a veil of ignorance that he proposes for purposes of moral theory, quite independently of concern about how we might conceive of a person's good. It is on this disagreement that I will focus.

Scanlon's basic objection[20] is with the interpretation of impartiality, but not only with what it means to decide on someone's good from an impartial point of view. He is also concerned that the procedure to be used in deciding on principles—that both do not favor one person over another and that one could accept independently of knowing what one's actual position is or will be—adequately respect the separateness of persons. Scanlon agrees that it can be helpful in finding such principles to use a procedure in which each imagines that he is in every other person's actual position in life (outside a veil of ignorance),[21] having that person's perspective on things, in order to see whether each person in any actual position could approve (or not reject) a proposed principle governing relations between people. While Scanlon does not make use of a veil of ignorance, his interpretation of impartiality implies that (i) if no person in any position beyond the veil could reasonably reject a principle on his own behalf, then (ii) any individual behind a veil of ignorance could agree to the principle. If someone from some position beyond the veil could reasonably reject the principle, then it could not be agreed to by any (in the sense of every) person behind the veil of ignorance. The reasonableness of rejection beyond the veil is a function of comparing the possible complaints to different principles of people in different (generic) positions.

Scanlon rejects the alternative interpretation of impartiality that Gibbard and Harsanyi accept, according to which impartiality is best exemplified by a single person deciding behind a veil of ignorance on the assumption that he has an equal probability of being in any person's position beyond the veil. The assumption of equal chances of being in any position is supposed to ensure that one does not choose principles that favor one position over another. But there is still no requirement that a decision maker behind the veil take account of whether each person actually occupying each position could reasonably reject a principle before he, behind the veil, decides to accept it. Rather, the order is the reverse of what it is on Scanlon's view: (i) if any individual behind the veil of ignorance would choose a principle on his own behalf, then (ii) no person in any actual position outside the veil could reasonably reject the principle. It is this Order Reversal, as I shall refer to it, that seems to lie at the heart of Scanlon's disagreement with the Gibbard-Harsanyi approach, for he thinks the reverse order is the wrong way to take account of the points of view of separate persons. He says:

> Whatever rules of rational choice this single individual, concerned to advance his own interests as best he can, is said to employ, this reduction of the problem to the case of a single person's self-interested choice should arouse our suspicion. As I indicated in criticizing Harsanyi, it is important to ask whether this single individual is held to accept a principle because he judges that it is one he could not reasonably reject whatever position he turns out to occupy, or whether, on the contrary, it is supposed to be acceptable to a person in any social position because it would be the rational choice for a single self-interested person behind the veil of ignorance. I have argued above that the argument for average utilitarianism involves a covert transition from the first pattern of reasoning to the second.[22]

In Scanlon's picture, the one person behind the veil would not conceive of the different positions beyond the veil as mere slots into which he might fall. He might imagine them as ones he actually occupies, as if he occupied all in order.[23] In this way, he is forced to think of all the different people who will actually occupy each position, which is what is ultimately important. Notice also that on Scanlon's interpretation of impartiality, one does not need to assume that *ex ante* one has an equal chance of being in any position in society, for one would have to check whether someone who is in a particular type of position could reasonably agree to or reject a principle even if there were not *ex ante* an equal chance of being in that position.

Scanlon also argues by example against the conclusion that an individual's choosing behind the veil of ignorance a principle that maximizes average expected utility bears on the inability to reasonably raise a complaint to an arrangement based on this principle. The example he employs[24] involves *ex ante* average utility being maximized because a principle will allow many people to receive small benefits when only a few will be very badly off. He thinks that the people who are badly off could reasonably reject the principle because no one of the many stands to gain much individually while others are very badly off, at least when there is an alternative that could greatly improve the worse off at a small cost to each of the many. Scanlon does not, however, commit himself to a maximin principle that would require improving the worse off, whether to a small or large degree, so long as the cost to each of many others did not reduce them below the level of the worst off.

Gibbard believes that it is only rational to sum the weight of considerations coming from each possible position into which someone may fall. Scanlon's example shows that he rejects this idea. Rather, he considers a principle from the perspective of each type of position that will actually be occupied by someone and compares its effects on a position pairwise with every other position in order to decide whether the principle should be adopted.[25]

I believe that Scanlon's example shows that attending to the maximal sum of utilities, regardless of what distribution of these is involved, would not yield the right principle.

Indeed, even when each of many persons stands to benefit greatly, it seems implausible to think that their doing so is justified when some will fare very badly. For example, suppose that Ida and Jay (the characters in one of Gibbard's examples) each prefers to be a master with the other being his or her slave. Higher prospective average utility for each can occur with slavery relative to a more egalitarian system. This does not seem to justify slavery or imply that we treat whomever is a slave respectfully even if he would have chosen such a system behind a veil of ignorance were he deciding from self-interest before knowing which position he would occupy.

Scanlon does believe that focusing on strains of commitment (as Gibbard eventually does) can do something to bring the results of his own and Harsanyi's versions of contractualism closer together.[26] I shall examine this issue further below.

One concern with accepting Scanlon's rather than the Gibbard-Harsanyi position on impartiality is that even Scanlon can accept that oftentimes an individual's actual (rather than hypothetical) choice to take a risk of falling into a disfavored position *does* undermine his complaint if he loses; such a choice can be a substitute for considering his perspective simply as a person in a disfavored position. Scanlon would have to explain either why hypothetical choice is different or in which circumstances risks are acceptable and in which not. Let us consider this and related issues further.

Gibbard has given the following example.[27] Many people commonly take a small risk of dying in a car accident in order to cross the road to get a chocolate bar (Chocolate Case). They do not follow a maximin policy. They each risk a big loss in a practice that results in each of many achieving a small gain. Presumably, a person has no complaint if he loses his bet and is involved in a deadly accident (i.e., no malice or negligence is involved). The question is what the willingness to take such a risk implies for risk-taking behind a veil of ignorance.

In order to make the point that use of the veil of ignorance does not take the separateness of persons seriously, it is sometimes said that a person's willingness to risk *his* having a bad fate for the sake of maximizing *his* own expected average utility does not bear on whether he may endorse a principle that risks someone else's having a bad fate for the same goal. (The Chocolate Case involves intrapersonal risk and benefit but risk taking behind a veil of ignorance can lead to interpersonal risk and benefit.) In one sense, this response seems misplaced. For, suppose it is the case that *any* individual—A or B—deprived of knowledge that distinguishes his eventual position from that of others would take the small risk of a bad fate for himself in order to maximize his own expected average utility. Then, when A suffers a bad fate while B has a good fate, this does not straightforwardly mean that A suffers because *B decided to risk A's* having a bad fate, for A would have taken this risk for himself.[28]

What must be emphasized to make the separateness of persons objection is the difference between one's *actually* (beyond the veil, not behind it) running even a great risk of death in order to have one's own chocolate bar and being willing to have someone else actually (beyond the veil, not behind it) run a risk of death in order that one have one's chocolate bar. In order for this difference to come to the fore, one must not interpret one's "being willing to run a risk to have one's chocolate bar" as including a decision behind the veil of ignorance to run a risk that one will die (if *one* turns out to be the person who gets hit) in order, for example, that one get to keep one's chocolate bar (if one turns out to be the *other* person who gets chocolate but could save someone else if he gave it up). Reasoning behind the veil of ignorance in the Gibbard-Harsanyi manner tends to assimilate interpersonal to intrapersonal sacrifice, and one might object to it on this ground.

So one could refuse, beyond the veil, to have happen to another what one is willing, beyond the veil, to have happen to oneself. Notice that the difference between self and other that is retained here has nothing to do with whether each person behind the veil would or could reasonably agree to accept the same risks. They each may be willing to accept the same risks behind the veil and yet still distinguish between (1) the case where they actually (not behind the veil) run risks for which only they may have to pay (if they lose) and (2) the case where they actually allow others to bear risks for them, including leaving those others to certain death rather than give up one's chocolate. This, I think, may be the way to understand the point of the initial response that we considered to Harsanyi-style veil of ignorance reasoning that said one might be willing to take on risks oneself for one's own benefit, but not allow others to bear risks for one's own benefit.

There is at least one more type of case that is relevant to the question of taking risks and whether respect for persons should be understood as treating people in a way to which they would have agreed because it maximized their expected good behind a veil of ignorance. In the version of the Chocolate Case we have considered, each person acquires his chocolate independent of whether another person is hit and dies in an accident. But we could imagine that it is someone's being hit that is a necessary means to others' acquiring chocolate. Behind a veil of ignorance, each must then decide whether to run the risk, perhaps small, of being hit, in order to have a good chance of having chocolate, knowing that beyond the veil anyone's acquiring chocolate depends on someone else's being hit. On Gibbard's understanding of contractualism, and of what it is to respect people, there is nothing intrinsically disrespectful about actually using others in this way that should prevent each agreeing to treat and be treated in these ways. There is nothing in his view that distinguishes this revised case morally from the original Chocolate Case. But ought we not to disagree with this view and say that the people in this case are contemplating treating each other in a disrespectful manner that rules out the agreement?

3. In concluding my remarks on his lectures, I shall consider in some detail Gibbard's case of the two fathers (which I call the Fathers Case). This is the case Gibbard uses first to drive home his view about how to reason from behind a veil of ignorance to a common goal that both parents would share. It is also a case he uses to show that it may be reasonable to reject acting on such a common goal.

In his second lecture, Gibbard focuses on the potential loss to each of the parents, A and B; he says it is worse for a parent to lose two children rather than one. He ultimately imagines the case so that parent A has one child at home and another in danger in a canoe.[29] Parent B's only two children need saving in the other endangered canoe. Only A is in a position to save anyone. Given this scenario, one possible state of the world would involve A saving his one endangered child, thus winding up with two children and B winding up with no children, having lost two. Another possible state of the world would involve A's saving B's children, in which case A winds up with one child and B with two. The second state of the world involves higher overall utility and also higher expected utility for each parent choosing from behind a veil of ignorance (on the assumption that each has an equal chance of being in A's or B's position). Gibbard argues that it is the utilitarian principle which implies that A should save B's two children that would be chosen by an individual behind a veil of ignorance seeking to do the best he can to further his own interests.

In his third lecture, Gibbard alters this rationale somewhat. The alteration involves his speaking in terms of a parent's "goal-scale" and maximizing the chances of achieving what is on his goal-scale, rather than speaking in terms of each parent's own good conceived of as his personal utility.[30] This change reflects Gibbard's worries about identifying a person's good and the possibility that a parent is concerned to save his children for reasons other than his own good, for example, from a sense of responsibility. Gibbard is also open to the idea that different parents' reasons for wanting to save their own children can differ.[31] I shall here speak in terms of personal interests in discussing the Fathers Case, but everything I say could be put in terms of goal-scales.[32]

(i) Let us now consider the second state of the world in the Fathers Case, in which A saves B's two children. Notice that it also involves the worst-off parent being better off than the worst-off parent in the alternative state of the world in which one parent (B) winds up with no children. This leaves it open that it is the desire to pick an arrangement in which the worst-off parent is as well off as he can be, rather than the desire to maximize *ex ante* expected utility, that underlies an arrangement that results in A's being required to save B's children.

Gibbard himself says that the choice of a principle for saving people in these circumstances is predicated on a parent avoiding the greatest loss.[33] He does not say that it is predicated on maximizing utility or saving the greatest number of children. Yet, he does say that it is the utilitarian principle that would be chosen in ignorance of who one would be. In these circumstances, avoiding the greatest loss and maximizing utility do overlap, but that is not sufficient reason to say that it is the utilitarian principle, rather than the principle that minimizes the worst loss, that his case supports. There might be other cases in which maximizing utility (and prospective expected utility for someone choosing behind a veil of ignorance) would require risking an outcome that is worse than the worst outcome under a nonutility-maximizing alternative. In such cases, the utilitarian principle would diverge from the principle that tells one to minimize the greatest loss that an individual can suffer.

(ii) Now consider another case. Suppose that parent B has four children, two of whom are in an endangered canoe. Parent A has only one child and she is in the other endangered canoe. In one possible state of the world, B winds up with four children and A with none, when A saves B's two children. In another possible state of the world, B winds up with two children and A with one child, because A saves his one child. Arguably, *ex ante* expected utility of each parent is highest if there is an agreement to bring about the first possible state of the world, as in that state a parent avoids the loss of two children rather than one, and we are assuming that each parent had an equal chance of being in the position of A or B. But the worst-off parent is better off in the second possible state of the world, for he has one child instead of none, and there is also greater equality between A and B because B still has two children.

Suppose all that is relevant is how things go for A and B (as this is how Gibbard discusses the case in Lecture II). Then it seems that it is the state with lower expected utility behind a veil of ignorance, but in which the parent in the worst-off position is better off, that is preferable, if we take seriously the good of each parent as a separate person. For it seems to me (and to Scanlon as well)[34] that taking seriously the good of each person as a separate person implies that we should be concerned with the eventual condition of each person outside a veil of ignorance, not just his expected utility behind a veil of ignorance. To derive this same conclusion using the veil of ignorance device may require us to conceive of the function of the veil of ignorance differently from the way Gibbard does. We should conceive of it as a device to get us to take seriously and compare pairwise the positions occupied by actual people beyond the veil, rather than thinking of those positions as slots into which one person might fall. This is a point Scanlon has emphasized and that I have discussed in section 2 above.

Of course, this sort of "maximin" reasoning could still result in the requirement that parent B, if he were the only one capable of saving anyone, save A's one child rather than his own two children in the endangered canoe. This is because B has two children at home and A stands to lose his only child. That the maximin principle has this implication is one reason to think it is also wrong in this context.

(iii) Next, suppose that parent A has only one child and she is in an endangered canoe, and parent B has only one child and he is in the other endangered canoe along with an orphan unloved by A or B. One possible state of the world would involve A saving his one child and B winding up with no children. In another possible state of the world, A winds up with no children because he saves B's one child and the orphan. If we just focus on the parents' own interests and responsibilities, it might not seem to matter much whether a principle is chosen behind the veil of ignorance that leads to one scenario rather than the other. But, of course, the loss to the children themselves should also matter, and given that they are the only ones who stand to lose their lives, it might seem that this is what matters the most, not the suffering of the parents or even their responsibilities to their own children. And, of course, an agreement on a principle that directs A to save the two children rather than one child maximizes each child's *ex ante* expected utility without violating a concern for making the worst-off position as good as it can be. (This is because each child would be as badly off as any other child if not helped and each parent would be as badly off as any other parent if he loses a child.) These considerations suggest that A should save the two children and let his one child die.

(iv) But the considerations that we have examined so far imply more. For example, in Gibbard's original Fathers Case, they imply that behind a veil of ignorance, an individual seeking to maximize his expected utility would agree to a principle that requires A to kill his child if this is necessary in order to save B's two children. Similarly, whatever supports the view that an agreement would be chosen that results in a requirement for A to let his child die, if this is necessary in order to save B's child and an orphan, would also seem to support the view that A should kill his child, if it would help save B's child and an orphan. It is notoriously difficult to see why killing and letting die should be morally different in systems that aim to maximize expected utility. And considerations that support the view that B should abandon his two children when he has two others in order to save A's only child, thus making the condition of the worst-off parent as good as it can be, would also imply that he should kill his two children in the canoe if this is necessary in order to save A's only child. For it is also hard to see why the distinction between killing and letting die should matter in a system concerned with making the worst-off parent as well off as he can be.

(v) Gibbard, of course, offers a reason why none of these arrangements that involve a parent letting die (or, I would add, killing) his own child would be chosen, namely, the strains of commitment. This is one part of his answer to a question he explicitly poses in Lecture III, despite his argument for a common goal-scale: "Is it ethically permissible for any of us to give special heed to our own special concerns and our own particular responsibilities? Doubtless yes, but why?"[35] Strains of commitment imply that one will care more for one's own child at the time her life is in danger than one will care for engaging in a fair reciprocal relation with others in supporting an arrangement that is best for everyone, and to which one would have agreed behind a veil of ignorance when seeking to maximize one's own expected good had adherence been expected. Before considering the idea of these strains of commitment, let us consider another approach to explaining the absence of the requirements to let die or kill that we have been considering.

Some might argue that a utilitarian perspective would not imply that A is required to either let die or kill his child in order to save B's children. This is because a parent who could do this could not also have the sort of strong love for his child that in most other circumstances, and overall, makes for better lives for parents and their children. So, those who contract for the sake of humanistic concerns and maximal expected utility would want the stronger form of love to exist even though it tends to lower utility on some occasions; they would reject the requirements to abandon or kill one's child. (This is a form of Motive Utilitarianism, a two-level utilitarian theory under which one chooses the motive whose presence will maximize expected utility overall, and then one acts from it even on occasions when doing so does not maximize expected utility.)

Alternatively, those who emphasize impersonal values might simply think that a greater value—superstrong love of parent for child—entering the world could be worth even an overall loss in life and other forms of utility, by comparison to a world containing only a shallower form of love that is compatible with requirements to kill or abandon one's child.

Suppose that the absence of a requirement to abandon one's child could be explained by such a more intrinsically valuable type of love or even a superstrong love that on the whole maximizes expected utility. The problem is that such explanations, like the strains of commitment explanation, seem to imply the absence of other duties that we have no trouble thinking actually exist. For example, suppose that A's child is drowning. The only way to save her is for A to kill B's child or children. A might suffer strains of commitment in living up to a principle that prohibits the killing (just as he would suffer strains of commitment in living up to a principle that required him to abandon or kill his child to save B's children). Superstrong love for his child might also lead him to kill B's child. Yet, this does not in any way diminish our pretheoretical intuitive judgment, or the tendency of a nonconsequentialist ethical theory to claim, that A is morally required not to kill the other child or children in order to save his own. An even greater strain of commitment for A might arise if all of his three children will drown unless he kills just one of B's four children. This strain of commitment might be greater than the strain A would feel if he were required to let one of his three children drown in order to prevent all of B's four children from drowning. Yet, this does not diminish our pretheoretical sense, or a nonconsequentialist theory's tendency to claim, that A is morally required not to kill one of B's four children to prevent his three from drowning, even if we also accept that he need not abandon one of his children to save B's four.

The fact that we commonly think that strains of commitment would not undermine the existence of a requirement not to kill another's child in these cases suggests that it is the *content* of the supposed requirement that A let his child die in order to save B's children, not strains of commitment, that makes this supposed requirement not be an actual requirement. Indeed, it suggests that there being no such requirement is primarily due neither to strains of commitment nor to the intrinsic or consequential good of having superstrong love that abides by no requirements conflicting with it.

Suppose, however, that strains of commitment were less in refraining from killing someone's child, when killing is necessary in order to save all of one's own children, than in letting one's child die in order to save someone else's children. I suggest that this would indicate that the strain of commitment we experience is a function of whether we antecedently think we are truly obligated to do (or refrain from doing) something, rather than that the obligations we have to do (or refrain from doing) something are a function of whether we would experience strains of commitment.

There is another reason, I think, why strains of commitment do not account for there being no requirement on A to save B's children and let his own die. It is often possible to coerce people into carrying out their duties, and doing so might maximize expected utility. It is not always true that utility would go down once we factor in costs of coercion. For example, suppose A knew that the state would be legally required to put his daughter to death if he failed to let her die in order to save B's two children instead. Then there would be no good reason for him not to carry out his supposed duty to save B's children. The state's killing a child who was impermissibly saved could also deter other parents from avoiding their utilitarian duties, and so it could be justified in a utilitarian system.

Gibbard originally says that he is concerned with finding a way to live with others on terms that no one could reasonably reject. Eventually, however, he seems to change this plan somewhat. He says in Lecture III that, on the basis of intuitions, he takes it that we should live with others in a way to which each would have reason to *voluntarily* adhere,[36] and "the way to live with people if one can, I take it, is on a *voluntary* basis that no one could reasonably reject."[37] But why, given his other views, is voluntary adherence to a rule or principle necessary, so long as people could not reasonably reject the possibility of being coerced? After all, we do not reject coercion in cases where we doubt that people would voluntarily adhere to a requirement not to kill another's child in order to save their own children. This may be a case where we think they will fail to do voluntarily what they have reason to do voluntarily, but it is not clear why, on Gibbard's view, the same could not be said of letting one's child die in order to save other's children. Furthermore, I argued above (p. 128) that it was not clear why Gibbard should take living on terms of mutual respect with others and living in a way that no one could reasonably reject as foundational in his system, rather than maximizing each individual's expected prospective utility. Hence, it is also not clear, given Gibbard's other views, why living on a voluntary basis should be important when some elements of nonvoluntariness could increase each person's expected prospective good.[38]

Notes

1. As quoted in Gibbard (Lecture I, p. 11).
2. Lecture I, p. 23.
3. Lecture I, p. 22.
4. Lecture I, p. 22.
5. Lecture I, p. 22.
6. Lecture I, p. 23.
7. Lecture I, p. 25.
8. Lecture I, p. 23.
9. Lecture I, p. 22.
10. All quotes in this paragraph are from Lecture II, p. 34.
11. In his "Contractualism and Utilitarianism" (1982), p. 128.
12. Lecture II, p. 42.
13. In Lecture III, p. 68, Gibbard himself allows that common goals that people have could involve impersonal considerations, such as

species diversity. He says that "coherence requirements don't rule this out." But it seems that on his view, these considerations are a part of morality only if people care about them. Scanlon thinks they are independent parts of noncontractualist morality.

14. See, for example, Temkin's "Equality, Priority, and the Levelling Down Objection," in *The Ideal of Equality* (2000).

15. In Lecture III, he replaces "own good" with "goal-scale," as we shall see.

16. Lecture II, p. 43; Lecture III, pp. 63–65.

17. This is the sort of tension between his and Scanlon's views that I referred to on p. 125.

18. It is also not clear why agreement plays a pivotal role in Gibbard's view of respectful treatment. He wishes to allow that a utilitarian principle that maximizes prospective average utility of each person might not be adhered to due to strains of commitment. Hence, it might not be agreed to behind the veil by those who could not count on reciprocal adherence by others or by those who could not reciprocate. But, presumably, these strains of commitment could be taken account of directly in formulating a utilitarian principle to which there could be adherence, without introducing the idea of agreement.

19. In *Utilitarianism and Beyond* (1982).

20. As he says in "Contractualism and Utilitarianism," pp. 124–25.

21. Scanlon uses actual generic types of positions rather than actual positions, but for simplicity's sake I shall not distinguish these.

22. "Contractualism and Utilitarianism," pp. 124–25.

23. Like the splitting-of-oneself device that Thomas Nagel suggests in his "Equality,"(reprinted in his *Mortal Questions* [1979]).

24. "Contractualism and Utilitarianism," p. 125.

25. He follows Thomas Nagel who, in "Equality," argues that pairwise comparison comes closest to being the correct way to combine people's different interests in an outcome. This raises the problem for Scanlon of whether his contractualism can ever allow the concerns of an aggregate of individuals to outweigh the concerns of a single individual when deciding on a principle. He tries to deal with this issue in his *What We Owe to Each Other* (1998).

26. See "Contractualism and Utilitarianism," p. 125.

27. Gibbard raised this example in response to my oral comments on his Tanner Lectures at the University of California Berkeley, March 2, 2006.

28. But I will return to this issue below.

29. Lecture II, p. 36.

30. Lecture III, pp. 64–65.

31. Lecture III, p. 66.

32. In his third lecture (p. 65), Gibbard also claims that if the parents do not choose a common goal-scale that will, from behind a veil of ignorance and assuming an equal chance of being in either position, maximize each one's chances of saving his children, then the parents could also be involved in a prisoner's dilemma. A prisoner's dilemma involves each parent actually winding up worse off with respect to satisfying his interest or goal-scale than he would have been if each had abided by the maximizing common goal-scale. However, in a one-time Fathers Case, a prisoner's dilemma will not result. (This contrasts with what results in the classic one-time case of two prisoners deciding whether to confess.) For if A were to fail to save B's two children in order to save his one child, he will wind up better off, in actuality, than if he had abided by a common principle that would have maximized his prospects of achieving his goal-scale *ex ante*. It is only if we consider multiple instances of situations like the Fathers Case that avoiding a prisoner's dilemma can be added to the rationale for each parent's choosing the principle that requires A to save B's two children in the Fathers Case.

33. Lecture II, pp. 36–37.

34. See "Contractualism and Utilitarianism," as discussed above.

35. Lecture III, p. 79.

36. Lecture III, p. 66.

37. Lecture III, p. 80.

38. I am grateful to Arthur Applbaum, Ruth Chang, Shelly Kagan, Jeff McMahan, and Larry Temkin for their suggestions on an earlier draft of these comments.

Reply to Commentators

Allan Gibbard

I thank Michael Bratman, John Broome, and Frances Kamm immensely for lavishing their philosophical acumen and energies on these lectures. Each commentator raises crucial issues and presses arguments in ways that require new thinking on my part. These are the ideal people to scrutinize my attempts in these lectures, and daunting though it is to face their critiques, it is the greatest privilege a philosopher can experience to have his thoughts subject to such attention so that he can come to understand matters better.

The lectures themselves were an attempt to join two sorts of inquiry. On the one hand, I inquired into the nature of ethical judgments and of normative judgments more generally. On the other hand, I engaged in ethical inquiry proper, making ethical judgments, criticizing and refining them, and investigating their bases. One question that drove me was whether the one bears on the other. Does what we are doing when we address ethical questions bear on the answers to those questions? The basic question in ethics is what to do, I claim, and this includes what social systems to support. Can this understanding of the nature of ethical questions and thinking help us in that thinking?

I looked in particular to a longstanding debate in substantive ethical theory. We depend on the moral motivations of our fellows to foster goods in our lives and to protect us from harms. Many of the goods and harms in question are morality-independent or "nonmoral," in that they are worth caring about apart from moral considerations. Happiness, accomplishment, and human attachments may be good examples. How much does the morality-independent good that morality can do explain the content and importance of morality? Fully, say "consequentialists" of all varieties, so that in this sense, morality is made for man and not man for morality. Strongly felt intuitions, though, seem to tell against such a view, ruling out acts that would be permissible or even required if what mattered about morality were exclusively its ties to our good apart from morality.

I asked in the lectures, then, how we should understand "intuitions" and their authority, and how this bears on what we should learn from moral intuitions. I did that by looking at two strands in moral thinking, utilitarian and contractarian. I considered the broadest questions of social ethics: These, I say, amount to the question of what kind of social order to support from an impartial standpoint. Possibly, our moral intuitions clash with utilitarian thinking because they respond to considerations that are contractarian, to what we would have agreed on as rules to govern our dealings with each other. I examined reasons to think that we would have agreed to promote a total good that encompasses the good of each person.

The commentators raise questions about both parts of this project. On the nature of ethical judgments, Frances Kamm discusses the nature and authority of moral intuitions, and John Broome and Michael Bratman both take up aspects of my own account of the nature of ethical judgments. On substantive questions of social ethics, Kamm talks of uses of a "veil of ignorance" to approach questions of social justice, and Broome takes up my use of theorems and their import for ethics. I'll respond to the points they raise in a different order from that of the lectures. I'll begin with substantive issues of social ethics: the import of a veil of ignorance and of theorems like Harsanyi's. I'll then turn to the nature of ethical judgments and the role of intuitions. That order best allows me to conclude with the question that I find immensely difficult but didn't much take up: Does the nature of moral questions really bear on their answers?

Veils of Ignorance

As Kamm says, I took it that "planning how to live with others should, at its base, involve planning to live" with each person "on terms of mutual respect." I preferred, moreover, voluntary adherence to a system for achieving this aim, if we can get it. Kamm asks why, and suggests that planning to live with others in mutual respect may be in tension with conceiving morality as a means of achieving morality-independent goods.

On this question of why, I'll only say that those were my starting points. I joined Rawls and Scanlon in proposing these as crucial aims, and I addressed readers who share the aims.[1] If these aims leave you cold, the lectures were not for you. I also joined in with Scanlon's proposal of a more specific aim, living with others in ways one can justify to them—in ways, to put it roughly, that no one could reasonably reject. I accepted that this aim might characterize morality.

Is all this in tension with conceiving morality as a means of achieving nonmoral goods—meaning morality-independent goods, "benefits that can be appreciated in nonmoral terms"? The point of the second and third lectures was to scrutinize a powerful set of arguments that this apparent tension may, on further examination, prove illusory. We succeed in justifying a way of dealing with a person, I would think, when we show him that it gives proper heed to his good and that of others. As for how the person's moral good figures in such a justification, the question needs more discussion, and I'll take the question up in due course. Initially, though, note that for whether a way of treating a person is objectionable, at least some kinds of moral good seem beside the point. It won't help, say, in showing a person that we are treating his good as we owe him, to convince him that we are seeing to his virtue or good character. We can't say "Fair's fair: True, I get the money—a crass, nonmoral good—but you get the virtue." Dismissing this piece of sophistry leaves other kinds of moral good to consider, but in any case, I fully agree with Kamm when she says, "the goal of getting agreement and justifying one's conduct to others is not a mere means to securing nonmoral goods" (125). A remaining question is how this moral aim cashes out—and that requires me to consider other things that Kamm and Scanlon say.

REASONABLE REJECTION

Scanlon formulates contractualism as a general position and then proceeds to develop it in his own particular direction. I myself followed Rawls in, first, adopting the general contractualism that Scanlon puts so insightfully and eloquently, and second, in specifying a way of dismissing objections as unreasonable—the "You would have agreed" retort, as I called it.[2] I then followed Harsanyi and expanded on him in drawing consequences from Rawls's starting points. (Some of these are consequences that Rawls himself very much rejects, but no one, I think, has found a way to make Rawls's package of theses coherent in its entirety. On this point, Scanlon and I agree.) We thus have three versions of contractualism on the table: (i) the general idea that Scanlon formulates and that Rawls and I share, (ii) the Rawls-Harsanyi version that I was advocating, which consists in Rawls's rationale carried through in the form that, I'm convinced, Harsanyi's arguments force on them, and (iii) the Scanlon version, which chiefly remains to be filled out despite his large book devoted to the project.[3] I explored in the lectures whether different sources of moral concern, contractual and benevolent, converge in their import. The argument that they do requires convincing us that the Rawls-Harsanyi specification realizes the insight of contractualism—something that Scanlon and Kamm deny.

As Kamm points out, I skipped past, in the lectures, Scanlon's discussion of Harsanyi in his classic article "Contractualism and Utilitarianism" (1982). Scanlon has many reasons for rejecting the approach to social ethics that Rawls and Harsanyi shared, but to my mind the interesting one is the one in his book, his challenge to the notion of a person's good.[4] Scanlon's earlier article was rich with illuminating insights, and Kamm reports well what Scanlon says about Harsanyi. I don't myself, though, find the article's arguments against Rawls and Harsanyi telling, and I owe an explanation of why.

Scanlon's chief aim in that article is of course to broach his own specification of contractualism. Although, for purposes of these lectures, I accepted general contractualism as Scanlon so wonderfully formulates it, I ignored Scanlon's own way of deriving consequences. One reason is that, as Scanlon recognizes, his own way requires reaching moral conclusions prior to applying any contractualist test. The general contractual test that Scanlon and I share requires as inputs conclusions about the grounds on which it is *reasonable* to reject principles. His own approach applies piece-meal intuitions directly to reasonableness, whereas I looked to a systematic test in the spirit of Rawls and Harsanyi. Scanlon himself rejects this aspect of Rawls and Harsanyi, and thinks that no more systematic alternative will be plausible. As my agonizing in the lectures over the legitimate place of intuitions shows, I can't reject Scanlon's way of proceeding out of hand. I worry throughout the lectures over what might distinguish legitimate intuitions from dogmatic pronouncements, and that indeed is a worry I find myself with in some of Scanlon's specifications of how his version of contractualism works. If, then, we can say something more systematic about what makes a rejection reasonable, clearly that has advantages—and I was arguing that Rawls had done so.

Scanlon's treatment of Harsanyi in "Contractualism and Utilitarianism" is devoted chiefly to distinguishing the Scanlon version from the Rawls-Harsanyi version. I agree that Scanlon's own position is distinct. Scanlon notes too that many of Rawls's arguments can be given within a general contractualism—as one would expect. That leaves Scanlon's actual critique of the Rawls-Harsanyi version. In the first place, as Kamm quotes, Scanlon claims that Rawls makes a "covert transition" when he goes from the reasonable rejection test to the test of what we would have agreed to. Now I don't think that Rawls exactly hides the transition from the general idea of hypothetical agreement to his own "original position" as a particular interpretation, though I'll agree he is sometimes obscure in explaining his motivations. The claim of a covert transition in any case can't apply to what I myself said in the lectures. I was quite overt in introducing the "You would have agreed" retort to an objection, and in delineating the circumstances where it would have force. It has force, I said, when (i) we are scrutinizing our going way of doing things, (ii) the situation in which the person would have agreed to the system is fair, and (iii) the motives for agreement wouldn't have been moral ones, but would stem from the very sorts of interests on behalf of which the person now objects.

There remains, of course, the question of whether the "You would have agreed" retort has force. I find in my own thinking that it very much does, but if the retort leaves cold someone who genuinely understands what it involves, then I don't know anything to say that would make the person responsive. We do need to be clear how the response works: Someone objects to proceeding by the established rules, but they turn out to be the rules he would have agreed to antecedently, before he knew whose ox would be gored, and the rules he wants applied aren't. He would have rejected the alternative he advocates, out of the very interests he now says are being short-changed. I myself find all this to be ample grounds to dismiss the complaint.

Moral Goods behind the Veil

Kamm and Scanlon, though, support an alternative way of glossing the "veil of ignorance" behind which moral rules might be chosen, a way that endows the parties behind the veil with moral judgments and motivations. The moral judgments the parties make behind the veil aren't, then, explained by contractualism; they serve to determine what would be chosen from behind this veil. What such a veil does is to foster impartiality in our moral judgments—and impartiality everyone in this debate agrees is needed. Also, says Kamm, "We should be concerned with the eventual position of each person outside the veil of ignorance," and we can see the veil as "a device to get us to take seriously and compare pairwise the positions occupied by actual people beyond the veil" (137). This amounts to requiring ideal moral judgments to be guided by full information and full and vivid realization of what is involved for each person affected. This too is a requirement that everyone in this debate accepts. The veil of ignorance test that Scanlon and Kamm advocate won't be controversial in itself, but it needs moral findings as input, and we can ask whether a Rawls-Harsanyi veil of ignorance offers a basis for the needed moral findings.

Some of Kamm's objections to the Rawls-Harsanyi test simply amount to saying that it isn't Scanlon's own use of a veil of ignorance. They are objections to keeping preordained moral conclusions out of the specification of what the hypothetical parties who stand behind the veil are like. I do not, she complains, "say anything about persons' demands that one plan to live this way with them." If an agreement treats people disrespectfully, she says, that should rule it out (135). People who are badly off could reasonably reject a proposed agreement (131). People behind the veil should consider reasonable rejection (130) and the risk of being treated disrespectfully. "One could refuse, beyond the veil, to have happen to another what one is willing, beyond the veil, to have happen to oneself" (134). Our question, though, is when an objection is reasonable and when it isn't. These complaints of Kamm's aren't relevant to a hypothetical contractarianism meant to explain the force of moral demands without assuming their validity at the outset.

It is of course legitimate for Kamm and Scanlon to argue that a Rawls-Harsanyi veil of ignorance fails to capture valid and important moral considerations. They can pertinently argue that the "You would have agreed" retort, even if true, won't show one's rejection of a principle to be unreasonable. Many of Kamm's and Scanlon's criticisms can be read this way, and so taken, they need to be considered one by one.

Kamm fixes on respect, and being treated with due respect is, I agree, a moral good that a person properly demands. Respect is a central moral ideal that both utilitarianism and contractarianism are meant to explicate, and if the Rawls-Harsanyi veil of ignorance doesn't capture it, it fails to capture a major basis of moral concern. We have to ask, though, what respect consists in. One aspect is an attitude toward a person, an emotional stance that portends constraining one's actions toward him in certain ways. Insults, undue familiarity, and the like express disrespect in this sense. The direct question for rules of conduct, though, isn't how to feel toward our fellows but how to treat them. Does hypothetical agreement from behind the Rawls-Harsanyi veil of ignorance fail to explain morally valid demands for respectful treatment?

It's bad to feel or think that one is being treated without respect, but that's a nonmoral bad, in that to see what is bad about it, we don't need to settle whether the treatment is genuinely disrespectful. Kamm's objection concerns being treated in ways that are disrespectful genuinely, and we have to ask what constitutes that. Not every action that goes against what a person wants for himself qualifies as disrespectful. Trying to get a job that someone else wants, for instance, doesn't ordinarily constitute treating him disrespectfully. What, then, makes a piece of treatment disrespectful? Kamm speaks of treating a person "as a mere thing," and others have used this phrase, but whatever it means, it can't tell against utilitarianism. Utilitarianism mandates taking each person's good into account in settling what to do, and this isn't treating the person as a thing in any usual sense. Kamm speaks too of "using others," but we use others every time we buy food or manufactured goods, and so the moral significance must attach to something more precise—like, perhaps, using people without their consent. We are left to specify what is objectionable by way of "using" people. Blowing up families, we are standardly told, is treating them respectfully if it is in pursuit of a sufficiently important goal that can't be as effectively achieved without blowing anyone up and if you foresee that you will be blowing them up as a side-effect of what you are aiming to do, rather than aiming to blow them up as a means to your goals. This may be right, but it does cry out for explanation. What makes such killing respectful?

Doesn't treating someone disrespectfully consist in riding rough-shod over his legitimate moral claims, treating him in ways we owe him not to treat him? If this is right, then in order to settle what constitutes genuinely disrespectful treatment, we need first to find what we morally owe people; we have to establish what constitutes due moral consideration. That the treatment is disrespectful, then, is the conclusion of a moral assessment, not a starting point.[5] Various moral theories tell us what we owe people, and hence what constitutes treating them with respect. Direct utilitarianism says that to treat a person with due moral consideration is to weigh his good equally, along with the good of everyone else, in deciding what to do. The Rawls-Harsanyi version of contractarianism offers another answer that may be equivalent: To treat a person respect-fully is to treat him in ways that he would have agreed to in fair circumstances for deciding how we are to treat each other. Perhaps neither view is right, but to establish what respectful treatment does consist in, we need to settle what we owe to each other.

DISTRIBUTION AND HARDSHIP

Scanlon and Kamm make other criticisms of the Rawls-Harsanyi way of filling out general contractualism, and we must ask if they have force. One might morally reject an outcome because it is ter-rible for some. (This criticism Scanlon shares with Rawls.) Some-times, though, we do impose terrible hardships, as when, in a just war, we order soldiers into situations where they stand a high chance of getting killed or maimed, or when we stay out of a war even though people are being slaughtered and maimed. We justly do such things, to be sure, only when the situation is desperate—but that's what utilitarianism would make us expect. Hardships and horrors for the few don't often buy widespread benefits, and a utilitarianism that draws on the experience of humanity will shape its strictures accordingly. In particular, with Kamm's own example of slavery, taking the possibility seriously that it might maximize nonmoral good would involve either a blindness to what slavery is like, or a view that our snap intuitions respond correctly even to fantastic situations.[6] Are a rational person's reasons for avoiding slavery not urgent if they don't include moral revulsion or a conviction that objections to it are reasonable?

Kamm says that I tend "to assimilate interpersonal to intrapersonal sacrifice" (133) and that I give insufficient heed to the "separateness of persons." I spoke in the lectures, though, of how the term "sacrifice" already assumes that one particular arrangement is the morally privileged default. I showed how heeding the separateness of persons doesn't tell us how to make tradeoffs. Rawls famously noted that ignoring the separateness of persons might make one a utilitarian, but it doesn't follow that heeding the separateness of persons will make one a non-utilitarian. As for questions of income distribution and the like, Rawls himself adopted a mitigated maximin standard for distribution, taking it to be the proper response to the separateness of persons, but Kamm rejects that. So how are we to think morally about distribution?

A wide range of standards for evaluating distributions of income, wealth, and the like can be analyzed as maximizing the sum of some index. I'll speak here of incomes, though whether it or something else is the best indicator of economic level is a complex question. The index will reflect the relative urgencies, from an ethical standpoint, of each difference in income. Suppose, for instance, that an increase of $1000 per year for an otherwise minimum wage family is as urgent as an increase of $100,000 per year for an otherwise median wage family. Then these differences will be represented by equal intervals on the index, and the ethical evaluation of an income distribution will go by the sum of everyone's index. The ethical view, whatever it is (within certain limits), can thus be represented by a suitably constructed index.[7] Distribution as measured by the index will be morally indifferent, but that is just because the index was constructed to make this the case. It has little to do with the substance of the ethical view that the index represents. Even if the ethical standard comes close to maximin, an index with this feature may well exist.

The real question, then, isn't whether distribution matters, but on what scales of measurement it matters and on what scales it doesn't. For income, utilitarians, Rawlsians, and many others will all think that distribution matters, and matters greatly. They may also, though, speak in terms of a scale for measuring income by its ethical import. As measured on that scale, they can't think that distribution matters, because the scale already takes into account all ways in which they think distribution matters. As Harsanyi noted, it is nonsense to think that distribution matters as measured on a scale if one agrees that the scale already takes fully into account how distribution matters. Utilitarians propose a scale that they think has this feature.

That leaves us with the question of how to assess the ethical urgency of income differences (or differences in whatever else it is that matters ethically in economic circumstance). If Scanlon's procedure yields an answer to this, it's hard to see how. Rawls, though, does have an answer, and he may still have an answer when he is dragged kicking and screaming into the format that Harsanyi argues is forced on him. For an individual, relative urgency can be read as a matter of the gambles over income that it would be rational for him to take on his own account. Tautologically, that gives an index of urgency that will guide him rationally in self-regarding gambles, as in such things as the choice of job or career insofar as his income is what matters in the choice. When one person's income prospects trade off against another's, the question, as Harsanyi's second welfare theorem showed, is how to calibrate their scales with each other. Each person's scale indicates prospective urgency from that person's own point of view. Should we use a different scale when the prospective urgency is ethical?

Once we take on board Scanlon's critique of the notion of welfare in his book, things become less clear. Still, though, we presumably suppose that income distribution matters because income matters in a special way to the person whose income it is. If, then, we can make sense of the idea of the prospects a person rationally prefers in light of this special way of mattering to him, we can again apply Harsanyi's second welfare theorem. The gauge of urgency is how urgent an individual rationally treats his income from this standpoint, and this is reflected in his "utility" scale. The prospective Pareto principle is then that prospects that are better on everyone's scale are better ethically, from the point of view of respecting each person and giving him his due.

Like things apply to saving children swamped in their canoes. (I focused perversely just on the fathers, though the kids are of course what chiefly matter in their peril. The point is that if the kids are *all* that matters, it's a no-brainer to save as many as possible. So I considered possible grounds for a father to favor his own, and that has to be something other than the value of their lives to themselves as considered impartially.) If the fathers, from the point of view where it matters which children are his, rationally find it especially urgent to save at least one child as opposed to a second or a third, then the Rawls-Harsanyi hypothetical contract procedure will reflect this as relative moral urgency. If a father doesn't himself rationally treat his saving at least one child as most urgent, why should morality?

As for accepting risks and imposing risks, a reasonable system of social regulation will of course treat them differently, for reasons a utilitarian can explain. A morally sensitive person could thus, as Kamm says, "refuse, beyond the veil, to do to another what one is willing, beyond the veil, to do to oneself." Implementation of utilitarian goals will involve permissions to treat oneself in ways one couldn't treat others without their consent. It's surely not *always* wrong, though, to impose risks on others. We do so whenever we drive, or whenever we cross the street. Even with the best of intentions, lapses are inevitable, and when you cross the street, a car you failed to notice may swerve to avoid you and injure the driver. The question is what ethical standards validly govern imposing risks on others. What standards would it be unreasonable for anyone to reject? The standards consist in a kind of golden rule, I would have thought. In the case where we are all in the same boat with regard to risks and gains, why not maximize our prospects for getting what's worth wanting in life—such moral goods as respect aside. It's not disrespectful to impose the risks we would all have wanted to impose and have imposed on us in order to lead a life of amenity. Even if we care about respect as much as we care about noninjury, amenity, and the like, we'll still need a standard for what respect demands, and it would be silly to think that it demands that, out of respect for each other, we all make ourselves miserable.

The Tangent Theorem

John Broome says that the theorem I invoke in the third lecture, the "tangent theorem," isn't Harsanyi-like, and more importantly, can't do the job I ask it to do. Broome knows more about the interactions between economics and philosophy that center around these issues than anyone else I can think of, and so I hesitate to disagree without having everything worked out in detail—which I confess I don't. But I'll sketch reasons for thinking that the tangent theorem, applied in the way I proposed, accomplishes more than Broome allows.

The argument, recall, took the form of a *reductio*. We suppose that a social contract C^* is the one that would be adopted, and that if it is adopted, each person will act to advance fundamentally different goals. Each person, that is to say, will have the policy of acting in a way that, given what he knows, maximizes the value of prospects as gauged by his own distinctive goal-scale. Since people are somewhat at odds in the goals they then pursue, the prospects that their interactions make for may be dominated, in that an alternative feasible prospect would be higher on everyone's goal-scale. In the diagram I used, there is a point on the upper-right frontier that they could jointly achieve and that does better on everyone's goal-scale. Indeed there will likely be more than one such point, but choose one, and call the prospect it represents the *ideal* prospect.[8] I then argued that they could jointly achieve this prospect by adopting a certain goal-scale in common, namely, the one on which the ideal prospect is highest among the feasible prospects. Thus if implementing a proposed social contract C^* would lead different people to act with fundamentally different goals—supposing their goals coherent—then there is an alternative goal-scale that they could adopt in common, thereby each doing prospectively better by the standard of the very goals each would have if contract C^* were in force.

Broome had a number of objections to this purported finding and the significance I claimed for it. I'll take up two of them first, because I find them the most troubling, requiring careful qualifications on my part about what can be shown and what can't. First, for all the theorem tells us, even if we choose a goal-scale to have in common, it needn't be "a weighted average of individual goal-scales." Second, "alterations in the feasible set will change the ideal point" and hence which goal-scale is ideal, and this creates problems that he specifies.

THE IDEAL GOAL-SCALE

For all the tangent theorem tells us, Broome says, even if there is an ideal goal-scale that we should have in common, it needn't be a weighted average of individual goal-scales. Now the argument I gave doesn't purport to establish what the ideal goal-scale to have in common is like. That's why I agonized over this matter later in the lecture. Rather, the argument is a *reductio* of the claim that there is no such ideal goal-scale. It starts out assuming—in order to refute the assumption—that if the ideal social contract were in force, different people would pursue fundamentally different goals, goals that can't amount to their all having the same goal-scale and applying it to different circumstances. I intended the theorem to show that this claim about the ideal social contract suffers a kind of incoherence. If the assumption were correct, this "ideal" social contract would be dominated, in the sense that there was an alternative to it that we can see must be even more ideal. For each person, that is to say, the alternative would better accomplish, in prospect, the very goals that she would have with the supposedly "ideal" social contract in force. For any prospect that isn't so dominated, moreover, there will be a goal-scale with the virtue that if everyone adopted it in common and coordinated suitably, they would jointly attain that prospect. (This goal-scale will indeed be a weighted average of the goal-scales we started out with, though not every weighted average of those scales will have this virtue—and of course as Broome says, joining together to maximize on the wrong goal-scale might be worse than working at cross-purposes.)

Broome's critique makes me realize, though, that I should have been more careful. I spoke of the possibility of prisoner's dilemmas, reckoned in terms of the very goals people are pursuing. I didn't show, though, that prisoner's dilemmas definitely *would* arise if people pursue fundamentally different goals, and I couldn't have shown that. I just said that they might. People might, though, be lucky and not face prisoner's dilemmas even though the goals they pursue are fundamentally different. What I ought to have said is this: First, *if* a prisoner's dilemma arises, then people would all have done better with a common goal-scale—indeed with any of a range of goal-scales, so long as they adopted one of them in common.

Second, even if no prisoner's dilemma arises, at least they wouldn't have done worse adopting any of a range of goal-scales in common. Again, doing "better" or "worse" is reckoned in terms of the very goals the person would have if the supposedly "ideal" social contract were in force. Probably too, I suspect, prisoner's dilemmas are hard to avoid when people have fundamentally distinct goals, except by fluke or in very special circumstances. I don't, however, know how to formulate this as a precise claim that could be shown true or false.

Broome mentions a different function that people might maximize to reach a given point on the frontier in the diagram. The function he gives, though, doesn't count as a goal-scale. A goal-scale treats probability mixtures of indifferent prospects as indifferent. (I took it that this is a requirement of rationality, and that people will be rational in the ways they abide by the social contract, and so will have goal-scales.) The way I set the diagram up, the indifference curves that any goal-scale gives rise to must be straight and parallel.[9] (Broome does point out, though, that the function he proposes handles the problem of non-convexity, which I myself leave unresolved. Non-convexity calls for more analysis than I can yet give it, but at this point I'll just say this: If it's only when the feasible set isn't strictly convex that we shouldn't act on a common goal-scale, that in itself is a surprising finding.)

I should also speak to another question that Broome doesn't raise. Isn't the argument I have given in effect Harsanyi's own argument, invoking his second welfare theorem? I require, after all, that the common goal-scale be coherent and treat what every individual finds indifferent as indifferent. Aren't these Harsanyi's exact assumptions? Yes, I answer, but in my treatment, these features emerge as conclusions, not as assumptions. What I assume is that each individual has a different goal-scale, as a result of adhering to a particular social contract. I then say as a *conclusion* that there is a goal-scale they might have had in common, such that their having it in common would have a certain virtue. Any goal-scale with this virtue must indeed satisfy all the requirements that Harsanyi lays down for "social preference" (or if it doesn't, that's because of considerations about a variable feasible set that I'll discuss shortly). But if it satisfies Harsanyi's conditions, that's a conclusion of the argument, not an assumption.

It may look as if the common goal-scale isn't doing much work. It only takes us to a single point in a fixed feasible set of prospects. It needn't hold steady as the feasible set changes, and so it doesn't operate as Harsanyi's "social preferences" do. In fact, though, as I am envisaging matters, the common goal-scale does considerable work. The parties who negotiate the social contract have very little information about the initial state of the world they will face. They agree to advance a fixed goal-scale as information arrives that bears on what the consequences will be. Each person, under the contract, applies the common goal-scale to many decisions taken in many states of information. As new information comes in, the prospects change, in his eyes, for how well his goals and the goals of others will be realized. Thus his prospective view of what the feasible set was keeps changing, but he goes on advancing the same agreed goal-scale. In consequence, although the map of prospects achievable by alternative social contracts looks simple and static, still the possible goal-scales that it represents each work across a vast range of informational states that, for all parties negotiating the social contract know, a person may be in at some point.

That's the reason I called the tangent theorem, in this kind of prospective application, "Harsanyi-like." To be sure, as Broome points out, the theorem is old news to any economist or applied mathematician, who thus won't find it particularly Harsanyi-like. In this application, though, it did strike me as Harsanyi-like in that, first, it is what is left when we drop Harsanyi's requirement that there be a social preference that is coherent, and second, it yields the result that a coherent social preference might better accomplish everyone's goals, applied as new information varies the prospective feasible set.

VARYING THE FEASIBLE SET

Normative theorists who think in economic or game-theoretic terms differ on whether the goals to advance in common, under a justifiable social contract that avoids prisoner's dilemmas, will depend on what's feasible. Harsanyi thinks they won't, and Gauthier thinks they will. My application of the tangent theorem, Broome says, doesn't ensure that the morally ideal goal-scale for us to have in common will be independent of what's feasible. In consequence, because of the complexity of life, we can't know what the ideal goal-scale is, and might well get it wrong. If we do get it wrong, then we might do worse, as gauged by the correct ideal goal-scale, than we did each pursuing our separate goals.

I certainly agree that having a goal-scale in common is no virtue in itself, if the balance of goals it represents isn't sufficiently worth advancing. There's a general phenomenon of the "second best," that conditions that characterize an ideal may not be individually good to meet when one is away from the ideal. That's the way it is with having a common goal-scale: Ideally we would have the right one, but a prospect that is top on a common goal-scale that isn't the right one needn't be better than another we attain without a common goal-scale.

As I say, the *reductio* argument that I offered doesn't tell us what the ideal goal-scale is. It just tells us that if a contractualist thinks that we shouldn't agree to a common goal-scale, his normative theory can't be right. (Any nutshell statement of course requires many qualifications, but even those aside, this is all the argument tells us.) I of course would love to be able to establish more about what sort of goal-scale it would be ideal for us to have in common, but that's a further endeavor. Perhaps we need to look further to Kant's vision of a kingdom of ends, but I won't pursue the full vision in this reply.

We do know roughly this: that if each person has a different goal-scale and the prospective result of their interactions isn't at the

Suppose, though, as theorists like Gauthier imagine, the interests that the parties to a social contract seek to advance don't themselves involve the relation of what happens to what was feasible. Suppose that if there is a morally significant relation between the two, it has to emerge from the contractarian argument itself. Then going sufficiently prospective in our contractarian thinking allows us to consider the feasible set as fixed. What's fixed, that is to say, is the feasible set of prospects as viewed by the parties as they negotiate the social contract. In another sense, as I said, the feasible set of *prospects* varies as the agreed common goal-scale stays fixed. The parties will learn many things as they begin to lead their lives under their social contract, including things about what was feasible and what wasn't. At the outset, though, they face a single, fixed set of feasible prospects from a standpoint in advance of all social infor-mation. The variability of prospects comes only at a stage where, for whatever reasons, they have already settled on a social contract to cover every contingency, selecting a goal-scale to have in common, and they start getting information that bears on what circumstances they actually face.

The argument I gave is addressed to a contractualist like Scanlon who rejects the Rawls-Harsanyi form of contractarianism. He takes as his standard of morally justifying an action whether anyone could reasonably reject permitting it, but he rejects the moral force of the "You would have agreed" retort in the form I support. It is reasonable to reject a social order, I took it in setting up the *reductio*, if one could do better in terms of the very goals one has as a consequence of adhering to its rules and rationale, and the same is true of everyone else. In my discussion of the possibility that what's just depends on what's feasible, I took it that we can push the question of what could be reasonably rejected to a stage where we don't yet have information about our society in particular and each of our places in it. One is aware, though, of the possibility that things will be as they in fact turn out to be, and is rejecting or allowing rules that cover, among other things, that eventuality.

frontier in the diagram, then by the standard of each of those
scales, adopting in common any weighted average of them
gives each of them positive weight will improve things by
standards of each person's goal-scale. It doesn't follow, though,
it will be an improvement from the standpoint of justice or d
ability. We didn't, after all, start out with any assumption a
what is just, apart from the assumption that is shown untenab
the *reductio* for the cases where prisoner's dilemmas arise.

Will the goal-scale to advance in common depend on w
feasible? That's a complex matter. As I say, I was imagining a s
contract drawn up and agreed to before any information c
along about what's feasible. Parties to the contract agree, tho
in their subjective probabilities for each way the world they
confront might turn out to be. (As Broome himself has sh
dropping this assumption stymies Harsanyi-style argumen
In the third lecture, though, I make no assumption that
party is looking to his prospective nonmoral good. They m
for all I was supposing, be looking to aspects of moral good. '
might, as Kamm thinks they should, already have a view
what justice requires, arrived at on grounds that don't inv
what people would have agreed to if they hadn't been motivate
considerations of justice. And they might, for anything I have
already be convinced that what's just depends on what's feas
(David Gauthier thinks that it does, and so do adherents o
Nash solution to his bargaining problem as determining w
just.) If, then, what's feasible bears on what's just, and if the
of hypothetical social contract that determines what's just
parties to the contract who are motivated by consideration
how an outcome relates to what was feasible, no theorem o
sort I was considering will rule this dependence out. What
feasible will then be a morally significant feature of any
come, and this even prior to bringing contractarian considera
to bear on questions of justice. On this score, Broome is perf
correct.

Should the argument have any force for someone who isn't even this much of a contractualist? It does amount to asking the adherent of some particular standard, "What are moral standards for?" If he thinks they are just for their own sake and that's the end of what can be said, it's hard to know what to do but walk away frustrated, or speak ad hominem to whatever moral intuitions he does have. The argument takes the form, though, that whatever is worth wanting, for each of us and with moral considerations fully taken into account, we could each better achieve it in prospect by all adopting a particular goal-scale in common. If someone is unmoved by this, I'm at a loss about how to pursue moral issues with that person—though perhaps we can find a way.

My Own Account of Normative Questions

None of the commentators are convinced by my account of what normative judgments consist in, and Bratman and Broome both focus large parts of their commentaries on misgivings over this account and objections to it.

COHERENT DESIRES

Bratman asks about wild contingencies. People act as they ought to or ought not to act in all sorts of situations, actual and hypothetical. Caesar's plight at the Rubicon was my prime example. I maintain that one's judgment on whether Caesar ought to have crossed is a contingency plan—even though one knows one will never face Caesar's plight. It is a plan for what to do if one is Caesar at the Rubicon. I maintain that contingency plans are subject to requirements of coherence. Bratman asks why this would apply to such "wild" contingency plans, to plans for circumstances one knows one won't be in. Why are even wild contingency plans subject to requirements of coherence, and desires, for instance, not?

I would deny this particular contrast; the real contrast, I say, is that the requirements on plans and on desires are different. Desires figure in a special way in planning and action, and the requirements on them stem from their special role. I desire to read quietly at home, but I desire more strongly to see the latest show, and so I go out. In this sort of way, desires weigh toward action. They have greater or lesser strengths, and the strengths of desires compose to yield one's preferences all told. The requirements of coherence that govern desires, then, are the ones that are needed for them to play this role.

Saying this requires some explanation. In the first place, the term 'desire' is used in various ways. "Desires" may be felt cravings, so that the feeling that one must keep an onerous promise won't count as a "desire." I don't know if such distinctions among motives can be placed on a clear footing, but I have in mind a broad sense for the term 'desire.' I count as "desires" any of the tendencies toward action that are resolved in deciding what to do, whether felt as a "beauty or a cutie," as Ogden Nash put it, or as a stern taskmaster.[11] Now I don't have firm views on the best way to construe desires in this sense, but here is one way it might go: A "desire," we can try saying, is a decision weight. It gives a score, in effect, positive or negative, to some feature that a situation can have. This score is the "strength" of the desire. This evening I give a positive score to reading at home, and a higher score still to seeing the show. I then use these scores to tote up an expected value of each alternative open to me, and in planning, I okay any alternative with a highest prospective score and reject any that is prospectively outscored.

Now of course, our states of longing, feeling obligated, finding a prospect attractive, and the like don't in fact come with precisely defined objects and strengths. Precise desires are ideal states, not psychic phenomena as they come to us. We need a better account than I know how to give of how an ideal role for a kind of state of mind can give rise to oughts governing it. Desires, plans, and beliefs, though, are all in the same boat in this regard. They will be vague and confused to a greater or lesser degree, whereas the story of their role will treat them as precise. The norms governing a state that have the flavor of logic rather than substance, we can now try saying, are the ones required for the state to play such a precise role. This applies, for instance, for degrees of credence as they figure in decision theory: requirements of coherence on beliefs, we could try saying, are conditions that states must satisfy to guide us to action in the way ideally characteristic of beliefs. Bayesian decision theory purports to explain the ideal guiding role of belief.

A desire is fit to play such a role, I'll try saying, when it is precise, and it is precise when it has a definite strength and a well-defined object. The logical requirement of coherence for desires, then, is that each have a definite strength and object. For a psychic state to be a precisely delineated desire in a system of precisely delineated desires, its strength must join with the strengths of all other desires to determine preference strengths all told among ways things might be. Preference strengths all told join in turn with degrees of credence in the various ways things may turn out to be to yield prospective scores for alternative courses of action. We have de-sires, more or less, inasmuch as we approximate, in our choices for action, the kind of system I have just described.

Not any possible state whatsoever that plays the kind of role I have described in moving a being would count as a desire. A robot might be set up to compute in the way I have described far more precisely than we do, but that might not settle whether the robot literally has desires. States of desiring need in addition to be like the states we know as desiring. Perhaps they need the same feel. The robot I describe will be as if it had desires, to be sure, but whether it counts as having them literally is a further question that I won't address.

Nothing in what I have been saying explains adequately how beliefs, credences, meanings, desires, preferences, and the like tie in with ideal models of them, and how this tie gives rise to logi-cal requirements on these states. Roughly, though, the logical requirements are conditions for the states to do the job the model lays out. They are requirements for the states not to be self-frustrating. Desires, for instance, have the job of joining with degrees of credence to make for preferences and choices. Many normative requirements on desires and other such states won't have this logical flavor. There are many things it would be logically coherent to desire but crazy. Desires ought to reflect what is worth wanting in life; otherwise they are misdirected. When, though, we dispute what is worth wanting in life, the dispute gets its content against the background of the logic of desires.

PLANS AND WILD CONTINGENCIES

A complete set of precise desires would determine a contingency plan for living that would cover even wild possibilities. The plan is the one that maximizes prospective satisfaction of those desires in each possible contingency. I spoke in the lectures, though, not of the desires that generate a plan, but of the plan itself. That gave me a less complex structure to talk about, and still allowed me to find states that match okayings and beliefs in oughts. (At least there will be a match for people who are ideally rational, and so fully prone to act on their normative judgments.) The formal requirements on a contingency plan, as on a desire or a degree of belief, will be the ones needed for the state to play its role, for it not to be self-frustrating. The role of a contingency plan is to okay or nix alternatives in various contingencies, thus narrowing down one's choices should the contingency arise.

Thus we can think of structures for thinking what to do and the like as coming in bare bones and more fleshed out versions. The bare bones version speaks simply in terms of a contingency plan. Some meat on the bones comes with a preference ordering that offers a rationale for the contingency plan: One coherently plans to do what one finds best. The full body, skin and all, comes with desires and judgments of reasons and their weights. One then coherently prefers what one finds more reason all told to want. Talk of all these levels, though, can be couched in terms of contingency plans. Judgments of reasons and their strengths, for instance, as Bratman reminds us, I treat as plans for how to weigh considerations. I think of each layer as subject to its own requirements of coherence, and I'm inclined to think that for the most part, we can understand the requirements on each layer in terms of the point of that layer. The point of a contingency plan, for instance, as I said, is to sort out what's eligible and what isn't in order to do only what's eligible. Bringing anything special about my own view of reasons to bear on these requirements, a stratagem that Bratman proposes and then rejects, may be superfluous.

Still, I much agree that all this needs much more work, and I don't know if this layer by layer approach to vindicating requirements of coherence on judging things okay, better, or reasons can be carried through. For one thing, if nothing matters, then everything is permitted, and it doesn't matter how one arrives at one's choices. The view that nothing matters is coherent though clearly wrong, but it make coherence superfluous. Mattering, though, pertains to reasons: Some things matter in that some reasons have non-zero weight.

Why, then, to return to Bratman's main question, settle one's plans beyond anything one might need? Often there's no reason, and when there are reasons they may be various. Plans in this regard are like beliefs: Many topics aren't worth forming degrees of credence on. For plans, one reason to make them that I stress is to help in setting one's standards. We can think about what matters in life by imaginatively confronting instructive situations. For the sheer logic of plans, though, what matters is not why to bother, but the things I have been discussing: what is needed for the plan to play its ideal role. Plans consist in ruling things out (where this includes ruling out ruling various things out). The requirement on a plan is that one not rule out everything, and the plan is complete just in case for each thing it covers, it either rules it out or rules out ruling it out. The direct point of ruling something out is to keep from doing it, but if one rules out everything one could do, this point can't be realized. Even in the case of a hypothetical plan for a wild contingency, the direct point of ruling something out for that contingency is to keep from doing it if the contingency arises. The occasion won't arise, one knows if the contingency is wild enough, but that's the direct point none the less. Ruling everything out that one can do in that contingency frustrates this point.

Oughts and Plans: Other Questions

There are reasons of a specially logical kind, then, to satisfy the requirements of coherence in one's contingency planning, even for contingencies that one knows won't arise. Bratman notes a kind of circularity in saying this: Establishing this requires thinking cogently in terms of reasons, but what cogency in such thinking involves and why is the very question at issue. This kind of circularity, though, isn't peculiar to my own account of judgments concerning reasons. It will characterize any fundamental thinking about standards of cogency. We have to be able to think already if we are to think systematically about thinking.

What is the "direction of fit" of plans and ought judgments to the world? Is it mind to world or world to mind? Both oughts and plans, in a sense, fit the world in both ways. First, both have a mind-to-world direction of fit: If a famished tiger lurks behind the door to the right, a plan to go left fits the circumstance, and so does a judgment that one ought to go left. A plan fits or fails to fit conditions; it fits whatever conditions make it the right plan, and an ought judgment likewise fits or fails to fit conditions in virtue of which one ought to do the thing in question. Both of these states of mind, then, have a mind-to-world direction of fit. Second, though, both too have a world-to-mind direction of fit: A plan's being carried out fits the plan, and doing what one judges one ought to do fits the ought judgment. There's a difference between these directions, to be sure:

Both with ought judgments and with plans, the world-to-mind tie is fixed conceptually, and the mind-to-world tie is not. Going left fits the plan to go left, and it fits the judgment that one ought to go left. These world-to-mind ties can't be disputed except through conceptual confusion. In contrast, though both the plan to go left and the judgment that one ought to go left fit the tiger's being to the right, and though the tie is obvious, it isn't conceptual. Alternative views of what the world calls for are intelligible, however crazy—for instance, thinking that the circumstance calls for getting oneself eaten.

It's another kind of "mind-to-world" tie, though, that philosophers might have in mind for ought judgments. We can gloss the "world" as including what one ought to do, and the judgment that one ought to go left can then fit the "fact" that one ought to go left—and the tie is conceptual. I can't object to this: It's a feature of the "world" that one ought to go to the left, a deflationary schema guarantees, just in case one ought to go to the left. And that one ought to go to the left isn't made so by one's mind. This contrasts with the plan fragment, "Let me go to the left!" where talk of a feature of the world clearly isn't in order and we can't properly speak of "the fact that let me go to the left." A remaining question, though, is whether this contrast is deep or a matter of grammatical form. Indicative forms embed freely and imperatives don't, and facts in the broad, deflationary sense are the shadows, as it were, of this grammatical form. Once we put "Let me go to the left" in indicative form—say, as "I am to go to the left"—we can say corresponding things about oughts and about plans. The plan to go left fits the "fact" that one is to go left, and the tie is conceptual.

Next, on normative disagreement: In *Wise Choices* I stressed interpersonal coordination. But though crucial to ethics, coordination may matter far less for normativity in general. Disagreement is the key, as Bratman says, and in the interpersonal case, disagreement must be understood as part of jointly thinking together, putting our heads together on how to live. Bratman gets my views on this just right. He then asks about impasses: If we face one, can we still think we are disagreeing? I find this puzzling, and I have spent parts of both my books on it. I think I want to say this: If it were clear where the impasses lie, would there then be a point to regarding us as coming up with separate answers to the same question, a question of what matters in life and so of what to do if one is you or if one is me? I could imaginatively debate the issue in my mind and imagine your voice as part of the debate on the question I am pondering. But I regard myself not really as disagreeing with you, but as disagreeing with the side of me represented by your voice.

WEAKNESS OF WILL

On this topic, I am uncertain what is the best thing to say. One approach I find clearly unsatisfactory: To say that ruling out an action in the course of planning is one thing, and thinking one ought not to do it is another. To say this leaves it a mystery why not to scrap all ought thoughts as having no clear content. It also means we could have two parallel sets of concepts, the plan-laden concepts that I describe and show, I think, to be possible, and then these mysterious but distinct ought-laden concepts. Why have both? Because of weakness of will, goes the objection to my account. Weakness of will is irrational, though, and so if we have ought-laden concepts as well as the plan-laden concepts that would suffice for all practical purposes, this can only be in order to give us an extra way to be irrational: form the conclusion that one "ought" to do such-and-such, and then don't do it.[12]

Don't cases of weakness of will, though, show that, for better or worse, we *do* have these distinct, normative concepts? They may not make any sense, but don't we none the less have them? Well, I'm not sure. People insist that, contrary to what Socrates thought, they do things at the very instant of being firmly convinced that they ought not to do it. They may, at the instant of action, change their minds about what to do at that instant, but they don't, they insist, change their minds about what they ought to be doing. Bratman speaks of having a second glass of wine while he thinks that he shouldn't. Now of course I do have to recognize this phenomenon, but what are we to make of it? Is he really having a thought with clear content? Perhaps his "ought" is not the general ought that I'm trying to explain, but one that takes into account a restricted range of considerations.

In my 1990 book *Wise Choices, Apt Feelings*, I worked to accommodate what such an objector maintains.[13] In the terms I'm now using, the approach amounts to this. Ought judgments are planning judgments, but not of the whole mind but a part of it, a part I called the "normative control system." It's the part of the mind that makes contingency plans. But when it comes time to act on a contingency plan one has, other motivations come to bear: fears, cravings, feelings of embarrassment or shyness, and the like. You think you ought to forgo the second glass, in that the planning side of you mandates forgoing it. This is the side of you that both looks to a situation regardless of whether you are now in it and motivates you when you are in that situation. Appetites, social yearnings, and the like, though, work on motivations right now in a way that they don't work on plans. Planning for a situation like your own right now, yearnings work on you but you say to yourself, "Sure, drinking more would be convivial, but in the morning I'll feel horrible. So when the time comes, let me forgo the second glass!" I still accept all this when the time does come. I accept, in effect, "When the time comes, let me forgo the second glass!" and I accept "The time has now come." The side of me that reasons what to do in situations concludes, "Let me forgo the second glass!" But appetite and yearning for conviviality work on me, and the totality of my motivation doesn't sufficiently heed the mandate of my planning side.

When I wrote *Thinking How to Live* (2003), I worried about whether it was psychologically realistic to think that there is a distinctive normative control system. As I might now say, my worry was whether there is a distinctive plan-responsive aspect to motivation, as opposed to responsiveness to craving, yearning, fear, embarrassment, and the like as they work on action but differently on planning for action. It seemed to me also that failure to think in a unified, coherent way is ubiquitous in our experience, and explains why we would experience some situations as showing weakness of will. It's not that there's some clear judgment of "ought" that we make which then fails to prevail in our motivations. Even if I'm yelling to myself as I start on the second glass, "I ought not to do this!" there's not something I mean apart from the injunction "Don't do it!" The timorous Penzance policemen sing, "Yes, forward on the foe!" even though, as Major General Stanley observes, they don't go. In a way, they accept what they are saying, and in a way they don't.

I'm not sure which is the better way to handle situations of "weakness of will." More recent evidence may support the line I took in *Wise Choices*. The evidence for "dual process theories" supports a psychologically real distinction between will power and other motivations.[14] Some might maintain that I could have my will steadily directed toward a policy, in my hypothetical thinking on what to do, and still think that I ought to do something else. I'll agree that there may well be senses of 'ought' for which such a thing is possible—a specifically moral sense, for instance. But I think there's also a "flavorless" sense of the term 'ought,' a sense in which what I "ought" to do is what it makes most sense to do, everything considered. This is the sense, I think, that Ewing identified. For this sense, I can't make sense of someone's genuinely believing that he ought to do a thing while steadily willing to do something else. If someone claims such an opinion, he either doesn't have this sense in mind or is oblivious to his real convictions.

IDENTIFYING THE ATTITUDE

John Broome has a somewhat different objection to my account of normative concepts. He thinks that my argument for the very possibility of the kind of concepts I describe fails, that I haven't proved that the planning states of my theory exist—except by helping myself to familiar normative concepts like OUGHT. In particular, he says, I haven't identified the state of mind of "okaying" an act, except as believing the act to be okay. He denies the independent intelligibility of thinking, hypothetically, what to do in a wildly hypothetical situation and okaying some alternatives while rejecting others.

Such hypothetical planning, though, it seems to me, is not hard to grasp. Suppose, fantastically, to use my stock example, you are forthwith to be Julius Caesar at the Rubicon, and now, in this frame of mind, think what to do. I don't find such thinking hard to understand. Rejecting some alternatives and ruling out rejecting others might well be stages toward hypothetically picking a course of action. (Indeed, it's hard to think why the subsequent stage of hypothetical picking, forming a full hypothetical intention to do one of the things one rejects ruling out, might ever be worth bothering with.) "Okaying" an alternative, in this hypothetical frame of mind, is just rejecting ruling it out by preference. Indeed in the case of action, if we can understand preferences, we can understand okaying and rejecting: To reject crossing the Rubicon, for the hypothetical case of being Caesar, is to prefer being Caesar at the Rubicon and holding back to being Caesar at the Rubicon and crossing. Such hypothetical okaying or rejecting may of course be idle—but it needn't be. It may amount to rehearsal for kinds of decisions one might have to make, refining one's powers of thinking what to do.

Suppose, though, Broome were right that attitudes like okaying can only be identified in the first place as beliefs. It follows, he thinks, that "if they are rational, they cannot help having the structure of rational beliefs anyway. Attitudes that are identified by their cognitive aspect cannot, if they are rational, help standing in the relations that rational cognitive attitudes stand in. The explanation of why they stand in these relations is that they are rational cognitive attitudes" (109). But this, I say, is no explanation at all. True enough, if someone becomes a murderer, he kills a person. Identified as becoming a murderer, we might say, he can't help but be killing. This doesn't much aid us, though, in understanding murder. Likewise, it's true enough that if something is a belief, then it has the features of belief. But that leaves everything to be explained—including how there can be beliefs with the "queer" features that Sidgwick, Moore, and others identified.

If I am right about how normative beliefs work, then to be sure, we should be able to identify ought beliefs as Broome advocates, just as by their subject matter, and to speak of aspects of the "world" that they are about. Almost trivially, dog beliefs concern doggy aspects of the world, and ought beliefs, if they are in good order, concern oughty aspects of the world. But how can there be beliefs with the features that Sidgwick, Moore, and others identified in normative beliefs? Are they perhaps just pseudo-beliefs, like beliefs about gremlins?

We might have thought we needed ought beliefs to figure out what to do. On an approach that identifies them as beliefs and leaves it at that, however, they don't seem needed. I can ask myself what to do, settle on reading the newspaper, and my belief that I ought to be working on a reply to Broome need have nothing to do with it—according to many philosophers. I reject any plan to hit my thumb with a hammer, and to do this, why would I need to believe, even implicitly, that I "ought" not to do so or that it would be a "bad thing" to do so? I just need the belief that it would hurt like hell, along with the absence of any countervailing beliefs (like that it would keep me from getting sent to a war in which I was likely to be killed or maimed). It's true that if I do what I think I "ought" not to do, I'm then "akratic" and thus "irrational." But that's no more than to say that I'm doing something I think I ought not to do, that lacks a certain feature. How does this differ from picking a car that I think lacks a certain feature, such as having a gremlin? Whence the special significance of the ought feature?

It's true that if you, like any of us, have ought beliefs, then you regard oughts as important, but this needs explaining. (Some philosophers think there is such a thing as an irrationalist who has ought beliefs but doesn't care; I myself think that any halfway plausible candidate for being such an irrationalist is just mixed up in his use of the term 'ought,' and doesn't know what he's talking about.[15]) Thus if someone asks questions about oughts that cry out to be asked, I don't find the answers that someone with this approach can give satisfactory.

I have argued, then, both that we can identify the attitude of okaying in an informative way, and that we are philosophically in a bad way if we can't. Is the mental attitude of okaying noncognitive? In my 1990 book *Wise Choices, Apt Feelings*, I did use that label for my theory of normative terms, but after that, I became increasingly puzzled about what the term was supposed to mean. (One eminent psychologist said, after some thought, "I guess when I use the word 'cognitive,' I mean it's complex.") As for normative "facts," in the ordinary sense of the term, there aren't any: When the detective admonishes, "Just the facts, ma'am," it isn't responsive to say, "The creep deserved it, and that's a fact!" In a philosopher's deflationary sense of the term, though, there are indeed normative "facts," if I'm right: "That pleasure is good is a fact" means, in this philosophers' sense, just "Pleasure is good." It's quite right, though, that in my explanations, I don't start out assuming that there are normative facts, even in a deflationary sense of the term 'fact.'

I do agree with Broome that there are two distinct, separately intelligible questions: "What shall I do?" and "What ought I to do?" which call for two distinct, separately intelligible sorts of answers: an intention and an ought belief. Here the question "What shall

I do?" shouldn't, of course, be read as calling for a prediction; it calls for picking an alternative. Now forming an intention or picking a course of action can, on my view, come in two stages: rejecting or "okaying" various alternatives, and then if one okays more than one, picking among the alternatives that one okays. The second, we can say, is forming an intention, and the first stage, on my view, pertains to ought beliefs. One needn't think that one ought to do what one intends; one may just think it okay to do and pick it, thinking one or more alternatives okay to do too.

Intuitions

I myself end up relying on intuitions, cautiously and critically, but I have two main sorts of initial worries. One is that even our strong intuitions turn out to be inconsistent. It's hard to see which intuitions, if any, can emerge undiscredited from the inconsistencies we discover. The second is John Mackie's worries over "queerness" and superfluity: Why think the universe contains the strange kinds of facts that we seem to intuit, when the psychology of seeming intuitions doesn't require their veridicality to explain our having the convictions we do and the strength of those convictions.

VERIDICALITY JUDGMENTS AS PLANS

My answer to the queerness worry is that the veridicality of intuitions, their de jure genuineness, is a planning question. It's a question of which of our convictions to rely on. Though it may be legitimate to speak of "normative facts that obtain independent of us," that will only be in the end and with a proper understanding. It isn't the place to start, I say, in explaining the psychology of our seeming normative intuitions. To start with "normative facts" invites the queerness and superfluity challenges, and leaves us with no cogent answer to these challenges. It's quite otherwise when we see that a de facto intuition's de jure status is a planning issue. You or I come to a view on these matters when we come to plan to rely on certain sorts of de facto intuitions. Settling on relying on a judgment isn't coming to have a psychological belief about oneself; it is coming to adopt a plan. I myself have plans along these lines, even if they are scattered and ill-formed, and I seek to put before readers and listeners considerations capable of persuading them to be comfortable with having such plans—but not too comfortable.

Frances Kamm, in a crucial way, doesn't quite get right the way I try to work all this out. "Suppose," she says, "there were no sense in which intuitions are genuine other than that we would decide, when we are in a state of full information, alert, dispassionate, etc., to plan to rely on them?" (124). I agree with her that the consequences would be untenable, but I myself suppose no such thing. The sense in which some de facto intuitions are genuinely de jure, I say, is that they are intuitions to rely on. That a seeming intuition is one "to rely on" is different from the psychological claim that one would have it in such-and-such circumstances, or that in such-and-such circumstances one would decide to rely on it. Claims that an intuition is genuine are part of planning, not of coming to beliefs about the psychology of planning.

I'm not sure whether my views on ethical intuitions should "give comfort to the many who ordinarily place stock in intuition." One picture is wrong, I claim, and if it guides these many, they should rethink. It's not, I say, that there's a unified, coherent way of thinking about ethical questions to which we confusedly respond and which we can bring to light by a method of intuitively supported hypothesis and intuitive counterexample. Our intuitive responses do often have rationales, but there is no single unified way those rationales fit together—no way that explains the shape of our responses. For one thing, our responses are inconsistent. The same can be said, to be sure, for our sensory responses, as with the

Müller-Lyer illusion where the appearances of length are shown false by measurement with a ruler. In the visual case, though, we can form a consistent view of the objective world revealed by rulers and the like, and this objective world enters into the explanation even of the illusion. (Quantum findings may not fit this pattern, but I'll pass over them in silence, since I don't know what to make of them.) We could try telling a story of ethical intuitions with some normative way things objectively are playing the role that geometric layout plays for vision, but we have too many candidates for what the objective normative world might be. Perhaps, as Sidgwick and Hare thought, it is hedonistic universal act-consequentialism. Perhaps it is some deontological pattern, as current philosophical opinion would have it. We have to settle what's veridical and what's distorted in our responses to the normative facts, and a psychological account of the workings of normative intuitions won't by itself yield an answer. We are learning more and more these days about how ethical intuitions work psychologically. They stem, it now appears, from a clash between at least two sorts of psychic systems, one utilitarian and one deontological—or that may be a good first approximation.[16] Which system prevails in a given case depends not on some standard that might be a plausible candidate for the objective truth of how considerations weigh against each other, but on such things as how close to the person one kills one is standing. Moral intuitions are not, in their psychology, responses— even distorted responses—to an ideal pattern.

I think, then, that we are stuck with a choice between intuitions as sheer psychic happenings with no status as information givers, and intuitions as I picture them. My own view ties in closely with the arguments of Sidgwick, Ross, and others for the indispensability of intuition in ethical thinking. Since we can't regard de facto intuitions as causal responses to their truth-makers, we should fix on their role in thinking how to live. Whether a de facto intuition is an intuition de jure is a question, we should realize, of what sorts of judgments to trust.

ASSESSING INTUITIONS

When it comes to killing and letting die, certainly our moral reactions to the two are different. That leaves us with the question of how to act in light of the contrast. We can ask ourselves how to treat the difference in reactions, and in particular whether to take it as a fundamental guide to action. I don't entirely know what to think on this score, but the following thought experiment seems to me to be highly relevant. Imagine we somehow erased our special horror of killing. Would we lose anything that we can understand independently of the special horror of killing, of our finding killing as such horrifying? We feel it's worse to be killed by someone than not to be saved by them, but experience equal, I find it hard to take this intuition seriously. But even so, as we all know, social prohibitions on killing are often highly effective but all too often not. Conditions where they are not are horrific in terms of the scale of deaths of people in their prime and the fear in which people live. Perhaps we can relax the prohibitions in special cases, but we'd better be careful not to undermine the special feelings of horror that protect us.

I agree with Kamm that an intuitive judgment "is no less objectively true if awareness of the factors and reasoning that justify it comes after the judgment than if such awareness comes before." I don't, however, think that this goes "contrary to what Haidt suggests" (121). My worries and Haidt's aren't that judgment comes before awareness of reasoning: We fully allow the possibility that Kamm points out. Haidt and his co-workers, though, find that, for instance, people cling to their intuitive condemnation of incest even when they are shown to their own satisfaction that all the grounds they thought they had were bogus. The subjects feel "dumbfounded." Still, perhaps they should think that there remain non-bogus grounds that they haven't been able to discern.

Kamm stresses that, as I would put it, de facto intuitions should spur us to look for a deep rationale that vindicates them. With this I thoroughly agree: There's a strong probability that a de facto intuition ties in with something well worth caring about. Once we identify a candidate rationale, we can think whether to live in accordance with it when it conflicts with other candidate rationales. We may, in some cases, rightly conclude that the rationale gets at something with an important bearing on how to treat each other.

Kamm asks, in my view, "What reason is there to think that one plan about what to do and feel in the realm of morality would be any better than another plan?" Well, first note that any answer to this must either depend on more basic claims about reasons and what's better than what, or have some independent plausibility, some plausibility that it doesn't get from a further claim. What's wrong with a plan to touch a hot stove? That I'd be burnt and it would intensely hurt. That's a reason. What makes it a reason, though? Why shun anguish? These aren't questions with further answers. To think this, I say, is to weigh anguish heavily against any course of action. Don't you agree with this weighing? What more is there to ask? To think this de facto intuition an intuition de jure is to trust such planning. Don't you agree with me to trust it? So what reason is there to plan not to touch a hot stove? The obvious one, that it would hurt intensely.

That's uncontroversial, I hope, and my own point was about what we are claiming when we say this. No direct gloss would be informative, but I can say what sort of state of mind this judgment about reasons is. It consists in planning to weigh anguish against a course of action. Its basicness consists in its not being rooted in something further to be done or to be sought.

Could I be wrong that it is bad to touch a hot stove? I am fixing on the most unproblematic aspect of how to live, and so for this particular judgment, I don't see how I could be wrong. On many matters, though, I might certainly be wrong. I might be wrong that human goods (and the goods of other sentient beings) underlie the valid demands of morality, and that the goods in question can be appreciated aside from being already committed to morality. I might be wrong that appreciating wonderful poetry is better than an equal, drug-induced appreciation of push-pin. What does being wrong on moral matters consist in? Truistically, it is believing what is not the case. It is, for instance, believing that with pleasure equal, push-pin is as good as poetry, when pleasure equal, push-pin is not as good as poetry. Beyond this truism, I can't say anything direct and utterly general. I hope, though, that I have said what it is to *believe* a judgment wrong. As for which judgments *are* wrong and how to tell, those are questions of how to live and how to think about how to live. Those are the kinds of questions I was addressing in the second and third lectures.

Metaethics and Ethics

That brings me to a question that the commentators don't address and that I find extremely difficult. Does the nature of thinking ethically bear on the content of ethics? Should understanding what ethical thinking consists in make any difference to our ethical conclusions? That's not a question we could answer on the basis of metatheory alone. My metaethical claims don't entail directly any normative conclusions. On the other hand, we can't antecedently rule out that the judgments we make will respond to our view of what we are doing, and that this responsiveness is proper.

It seems to us clear we shouldn't push a person in front of a trolley even to save five people with certainty. We know now that making this judgment is a result of emotional centers in the brain overpowering centers that operate in a more or less utilitarian way, and that these emotional centers are highly responsive to such matters as how close one is to the person one kills. Also, in ways that haven't been studied neurologically so far as I know, the brain delivers a firm judgment that sheer literal nearness isn't morally relevant. Everyone agrees that a strong emotional revulsion to close-range killing is a good thing for us to have—even if that's only because it works, mostly, to correct for such things as wishful thinking and misjudgments of evidence that can distort utilitarian calculations. Our question concerns our revulsion-infused judgment tendencies to rule out this instance of killing to save. Are they intimations of wrongness even if for no further reason? Or are they useful emergency danger signals, good for the most part in keeping us on the right path, but sending the wrong message in this particular instance?

That's one question, but now I'm asking a further question *about* this one. Should it make any difference which of the following two our question is? (i) whether the emotional response is an indication of wrongness in the way, say, that arithmetic judgments respond to how things are with numbers, or (ii) whether to give the response fundamental weight in our thinking how to deal with each other. Nothing rules out conceptually an answer of either yes or no to this question of whether the nature of intuitions bears on how to assess them. As a matter of sheer conceptual requirements, anything at all might bear on what to do and what to weigh toward doing things. Still, once we put our ethical questions as ones of what to do and how to feel about things we can do, we may take up substantive questions of ethics in a different frame of mind.

We feel the wrongness of killing more strongly than we feel the wrongness of letting a person die, even when that clearly is the only difference that could matter. This difference in our responses is probably a good thing, and if it indicates the special wrongness of killing whether or not we can find some further ground for abhorrence, we'd better take heed. If, though, the question is what to do and why, we may find the fundamental import of the kill/let-die distinction more suspect. True, we'll have to take some things as basic grounds for action, but why this? Someone is just as dead in either case; indeed we have stipulated that there is no reason to treat the two actions differently *except* whatever it is that makes one a case of killing and the other a case of letting die. First, then, why care if you are the one who will in either case be dead? And second, if there's no good answer to this, why care if you are the one who must choose to kill one or let the other die? That being alive and the things it allows matter is likewise an intuition, true enough, but it isn't one that melts away if the question becomes what to want and why, what considerations to weigh for and against actions, and what responses to treat as guides to action. Intuitions treated as visions of how things stand morally, in contrast, aren't as open to the challenge "Why on earth heed that?" as are seeming answers to what to want and why. Seeing the question as how to live and the grounds for answers as ordinary facts may make us more attuned to what really matters in the ways we treat each other.

Notes

1. Rawls, *A Theory of Justice* (1971); Scanlon, "Contractualism and Utilitarianism" (1982) and *What We Owe to Each Other* (1998).

2. Harsanyi, "Morality and the Theory of Rational Behavior" (1977).

3. Scanlon, *What We Owe* (1998).

4. Scanlon, *What We Owe* (1998), chap. 2.

5. See Frankena, "The Ethics of Respect for Persons" (1986).

6. See Hare, "What Is Wrong with Slavery." A onetime slave himself, Hare examines a sort of case in which utilitarianism might really endorse slavery.

7. Technically, the requirement for such an index to be possible is "separability," but what this amounts to I won't go into.

8. A point in the diagram may represent more than one prospect, and that is a matter that requires more analysis. A point represents all prospects that are indifferent to a given prospect on the goal-scales of everyone. But I'll speak as though each point in the diagram represents a single prospect, leaving the needed further analysis for other occasions.

9. The argument is this: The axes are goal-scales, and so on them, probability mixtures of indifferent prospects are indifferent. It will follow that for any possible goal-scale, indifference according

to that scale will be represented by a straight line. Take any two prospects that are indifferent as gauged by goal-scale U. Then probability mixtures of them are indifferent. All probability mixtures, though, lie along a straight line in the diagram. Take, for instance, an even probability mixture of prospects a and b. Its x coordinate lies halfway between a and b on goal-scale U_1, and its y coordinate lies halfway between a and b on goal-scale U_2, and so the point lies halfway between on the line segment joining them.

10. Broome's "probability agreement theorem," *Weighing Goods* (1991), p. 160.

11. Ogden Nash wrote, "Oh, duty, duty—Why hast thou not the visage of a sweetie, or a cutie?" and David Gauthier used this as an epigram for his own theory of duty in *Morals by Agreement* (1986).

12. Scanlon thinks there are uses for a distinct ought concept; see his "Metaphysics and Morals" (2003) and "Reasons and Decisions" (2006) with my "Reply to Critics" (2006).

13. In my treatment of weakness of will in the book, I was responding to challenges Bratman pressed on me in a wonderful series of lunchtime conversations we had while I was first writing the book.

14. I thank Chandra Sripada for calling my attention to these developments; see his "Weakness of Will and the Divided Mind" (manuscript in preparation). See also Chaiken and Trope, *Dual Process Theories* (1979). Howard Nye has also urged that I should stick to the *Wise Choices* account of weakness of will.

15. See Lenman, "The Externalist and the Amoralist" (1999) and my *Thinking How to Live* (2003), p. 12.

16. Greene et al. (2004), "The Neural Bases of Cognitive Conflict and Control in Moral Judgment."

Frankena, W. K., (1986). "The Ethics of Respect for Persons." *Philosophical Topics* 14: 149–67.

Gauthier, David (1982). "On the Refutation of Utilitarianism." In Harlan B. Miller and William H. Williams, eds., *The Limits of Utilitarianism* (Minneapolis: University of Minnesota Press).

Gauthier, David (1986). *Morals by Agreement* (Oxford: Oxford University Press).

Gauthier, David (1991). *Morals by Agreement* (New York: Cambridge University Press).

Gibbard, Allan (1971). *Utilitarianisms and Coordination* (Reprint, New York: Garland, 1990).

Gibbard, Allan (1976). "Natural Property Rights." *Nous* 10: 77–88.

Gibbard, Allan (1978). "Act-Utilitarian Agreements." In Alvin Goldman and Jaegwon Kim, eds., *Values and Morals* (Dordrecht, Holland: Reidel).

Gibbard, Allan (1979). "Disparate Goods and Rawls' Difference Principle: A Social Choice Theoretic Treatment." *Theory and Decision* 11: 267–88.

Gibbard, Allan (1986). "Interpersonal Comparisons: Preference, Good, and the Intrinsic Reward of a Life." In J. Elster and A. Hylland, eds., *The Foundations of Social Choice Theory* (Cambridge, England: Cambridge University Press).

Gibbard, Allan (1990). *Wise Choices, Apt Feelings: A Theory of Normative Judgment* (Cambridge, Mass.: Harvard University Press; and Oxford: Oxford University Press).

Gibbard, Allan (1999). "Morality As Consistency in Living: Korsgaard's Kantian Lectures." *Ethics* 110: 140–64.

Gibbard, Allan (2002). "Knowing What to Do, Seeing What to Do." In Philip Stratton-Lake, ed., *Ethical Intuitionism: Re-Evaluations* (Oxford: Clarendon Press).

Gibbard, Allan (2003). *Thinking How to Live* (Cambridge, Mass.: Harvard University Press).

Gibbard, Allan (2006). "Moral Feelings and Moral Concepts." In Russ Schafer-Landau, ed., *Oxford Studies in Metaethics*, vol.1 (Oxford: Oxford University Press).

Bibliography

Binmore, Ken (1994). *Playing Fair: Game Theory and the Social Contract*, vol. 1 (Cambridge, Mass.: MIT Press).

Brandt, Richard (1963). "Toward a Credible Form of Utilitarianism." In Hector-Neri Castaneda and George Nakhnikian, eds., *Morality and the Language of Conduct* (Detroit: Wayne State University Press).

Brandt, Richard (1967). "Some Merits of One Form of Rule Utilitarianism." *University of Colorado Studies in Philosophy*, vol. 3 (Boulder: University of Colorado Press), pp. 39–65.

Brandt, Richard B. (1979). *A Theory of the Good and the Right* (Oxford: Clarendon Press).

Bratman, Michael (1987, 1999). *Intention, Plans, and Practical Reason* (Cambridge, Mass.: Harvard University Press, 1987; reissued by CSLI Publications, 1999).

Bratman, Michael (2006). "*Thinking How to Live* and the Restriction Problem." *Philosophy and Phenomenological Research* 72, 3 (May): 708–14.

Bratman, Michael (forthcoming). "Intention, Belief, Practical, Theoretical." In Jens Timmerman, John Skorupski, and Simon Robertson, eds., *Spheres of Reason*.

Broome, John (1991). *Weighing Goods: Equality, Uncertainty and Time* (Oxford: Blackwell Publishers).

Broome, John (2005). "Does Rationality Give Us Reasons?" *Philosophical Issues* 15: 321–37.

Chaiken, Shelly, and Trope, Yaacov (1999). *Dual-Process Theories in Social Psychology* (New York: Guilford Publications).

Fiske, Alan Page (1992). "The Four Elementary Forms of Sociality: Framework for a Unified Theory of Social Relations." *Psychological Review* 99: 689–723.

Frankena, W. K. (1963). *Ethics* (Englewood Cliffs, NJ: Prentice-Hall).

Gibbard, Allan (2006). "Reply to Critics." *Philosophy and Phenomenological Research* 72, 3 (May): 730–45.

Greene, Joshua D., Nystrom, L., Engell, A. D., Darley, J. M., and Cohen, J. D. (2004). "The Neural Bases of Cognitive Conflict and Control in Moral Judgment." *Neuron* 44 (October 14): 389–400.

Griffin, James (1986). *Well-Being: Its Meaning, Measurement, and Moral Importance* (Oxford: Oxford University Press).

Haidt, Jonathan (2001). "The Emotional Dog and Its Rational Tail: A Social Intuitionist Approach to Moral Judgments." *Psychological Review* 108, 4: 814–34.

Hammond, Peter (1988). "Consequentialist Foundations for Expected Utility." *Theory and Decision* 25: 25–78.

Hare, R. M. (1979). "What Is Wrong with Slavery." *Philosophy and Public Affairs* 8, 2 (winter): 103–21.

Hare, R. M. (1993). "Could Kant Have Been a Utilitarian?" *Utilitas* 5, 1 (May): 243–64.

Harsanyi, John (1953). "Cardinal Utility in Welfare Economics and in the Theory of Risk-Taking." *Journal of Political Economy* 61: 434–35.

Harsanyi, John (1955). "Cardinal Welfare, Individualistic Ethics, and Interpersonal Comparisons of Utility." *Journal of Political Economy* 63: 309–21.

Harsanyi, John (1977). "Morality and the Theory of Rational Behavior." *Social Research* 44, 4: 623–56.

Jeske, Diane, and Fumerton, Richard (1997). "Relatives and Relativism." *Philosophical Studies* 87: 143–57.

Kahneman, Daniel, Knetsch, J. L., and Thaler, R. H. (1990). "Experimental Tests of the Endowment Effect and the Coase Theorem." *Journal of Political Economy* 98: 1325–48.

Kahneman, Daniel, and Tversky, Amos (1979). "Prospect Theory: An Analysis of Decision under Risk." *Econometrica* 47: 263–91.

Kant, Immanuel (1785). *Grundlegung der Metaphysic der Sitten* (Riga: Hartknoch). Trans. as *Foundations of the Metaphysics of Morals*, Lewis White Beck (Indianapolis, Ind.: Bobbs-Merrill, 1959). Standard page numbers from the Königliche

Preussische Akademie der Wissenschaft edition (Berlin, 1902–1938).

Korsgaard, Christine M. (1996). *The Sources of Normativity* (Cambridge, England: Cambridge University Press).

Lenman, James (1999). "The Externalist and the Amoralist." *Philosophia* 27: 441–57.

Mackie, John L. (1977). *Ethics: Inventing Right and Wrong* (Harmondsworth, England: Penguin Books).

Marcus, Gary (2004). *The Birth of the Mind* (New York: Basic Books).

McClennen, Edward F. (1990). *Rationality and Dynamic Choice* (Cambridge, England: Cambridge University Press).

Moore, G. E. (1903). *Principia Ethica* (Cambridge, England: Cambridge University Press).

Nagel, Thomas (1979). *Mortal Questions* (New York: Cambridge University Press).

Nozick, Robert (1974). *Anarchy, State, and Utopia.* (New York: Basic Books).

Ramsey, Frank Plumpton (1931). "Truth and Probability." *The Foundations of Mathematics and Other Logical Essays* (London: Routledge & Kegan Paul).

Rawls, John (1971). *A Theory of Justice* (Cambridge, Mass.: Harvard University Press).

Rawls, John (1977). "The Basic Structure As Subject." *American Philosophical Quarterly* 14, 2: 159–65.

Ross, W. D. (1930). *The Right and the Good* (Oxford: Clarendon Press).

Savage, Leonard J. (1954, 1972). *The Foundations of Statistics*, 2nd ed. (New York: Dover).

Scanlon, T. M. (1982). "Contractualism and Utilitarianism." In Amartya Sen and Bernard Williams, eds., *Utilitarianism and Beyond* (Cambridge, England: Cambridge University Press).

Scanlon, T. M. (1998). "The Status of Well-Being." In G. B. Peterson, ed., *The Tanner Lectures on Human Values* (Salt Lake City: University of Utah Press).

Scanlon, T. M. (1998). *What We Owe to Each Other* (Cambridge, Mass.: Harvard University Press).

Scanlon, T. M. (2003). "Metaphysics and Morals." *Proceedings and Addresses of the American Philosophical Association* 77, 2 (November): 7–22.

Scanlon, T. M. (2006). "Reasons and Decisions." *Philosophy and Phenomenological Research* 72, 3 (May): 723–29.

Sen, Amartya K. (1985). "Rationality and Uncertainty." *Theory and Decision* 18, 2: 109–27.

Sidgwick, Henry (1907). *The Methods of Ethics,* 7th ed. (London: Macmillan).

Smith, Holly M. (1980). "Rawls and Utilitarianism." In *John Rawls' Theory of Social Justice,* Gene Blocker and Elizabeth Smith, eds. (Columbus: Ohio University Press).

Sripada, Chandra (submitted). "Weakness of Will and the Divided Mind."

Suzumura, Kotaro (1997). "Interpersonal Comparisons of the Extended Sympathy Type and the Possibility of Social Choice." In Kenneth J. Arrow, Amartya K. Sen, and Kotaro Suzumura, eds., *Social Choice Re-Examined,* vol. 2 (New York: St. Martin's Press).

Temkin, Larry S. (2000). "Equality, Priority, and the Levelling Down Objection." In Matthew Clayton and Andrew Williams, eds., *The Ideal of Equality* (New York: MacMillan and St. Martin's Press).

Thaler, R. (1980). "Towards a Positive Theory of Consumer Choice." *Journal of Economic Behavior and Organization* 1: 39–60.

Tversky, A., and Kahneman, D. (1981). "The Framing of Decisions and the Psychology of Choice." *Science* 211: 453–58.

Varian, Hal R. (1975). "Distributive Justice, Welfare Economics, and the Theory of Fairness." *Philosophy and Public Affairs* 4, 3: 223–47.

Index

The letter *f* following a page number denotes a figure.